COOKING WITH
SALMON

COOKING WITH
SALMON
THE KING OF FISH

CONSULTANT EDITOR
JANE BAMFORTH

LORENZ BOOKS

This edition is published by Lorenz Books
Lorenz Books is an imprint of Anness Publishing Ltd,
Hermes House, 88-89 Blackfriars Road, London SE1 8HA
tel. 020 7401 2077; fax 020 7633 9499; www.lorenzbooks.com; info@anness.com
© Anness Publishing Ltd 2003

This edition distributed in the UK by The Manning Partnership Ltd, 6 The Old Dairy, Melcombe Road,
Bath BA2 3LR; tel. 01225 478 444; fax 01225 478 440; sales@manning-partnership.co.uk
This edition distributed in the USA and Canada by National Book Network, 4720 Boston Way, Lanham,
MD 20706; tel. 301 459 3366; fax 301 459 1705; www.nbnbooks.com
This edition distributed in Australia by Pan Macmillan Australia, Level 18, St Martins Tower, 31 Market St,
Sydney, NSW 2000; tel. 1300 135 113; fax 1300 135 103; customer.service@macmillan.com.au

A CIP catalogue record for this book is available from the British Library.

PUBLISHER: Joanna Lorenz
MANAGING EDITOR: Judith Simons
PROJECT EDITOR: Sarah Ainley
COPY EDITOR: Jenni Fleetwood
REFERENCE SECTION: Jenni Fleetwood and Kate Whiteman
RECIPES: Catherine Atkinson, Alex Barker, Jane Bamforth, Carla Capalbo, Jacqueline Clarke,
Roz Denny, Matthew Drennan, Joanne Farrow, Christine France, Brian Glover, Becky Johnson,
Christine Ingram, Liz Trigg, Linda Tubby, Kate Whiteman and Elizabeth Wolf-Cohen
PHOTOGRAPHY: Tim Auty, Martin Brigdale, Nicki Dowey, James Duncan, Michelle Garrett,
Dave Jordan, David King, Thomas Odulate, William Lingwood and Sam Stowell
ADDITIONAL PHOTOGRAPHY (pp8 and 9): The Anthony Blake Photo Library
DESIGNER: Adelle Morris
INDEXER: Helen Snaith
PRODUCTION CONTROLLER: Claire Rae

1 3 5 7 9 10 8 6 4 2

NOTES

Bracketed terms are intended for American readers.
For all recipes, quantities are given in both metric and imperial measures and, where appropriate,
measures are also given in standard cups and spoons. Follow one set, but not a mixture, because
they are not interchangeable.
Standard spoon and cup measures are level. 1 tsp = 5ml, 1 tbsp = 15ml, 1 cup = 250ml/8fl oz
Australian standard tablespoons are 20ml. Australian readers should use 3 tsp in place of 1 tbsp for
measuring small quantities of gelatine, cornflour, salt, etc.
Medium eggs (US large) are used unless otherwise stated.

CONTENTS

INTRODUCTION

Lovely to look at, delicious and nutritious, salmon makes it a pure pleasure to eat more fish.

Fresh salmon can be served in dozens of different ways - poached, baked, steamed, fried,

grilled (broiled), cooked on the barbecue or in the microwave. Equally delicious hot or cold,

it also stars in soufflés and mousses, pastries and pasta dishes, sandwiches and salads. Salmon

tastes superb as sushi or sashimi, and it can be smoked successfully, adding another dimension

to its culinary possibilities. The tasty, varied recipes in this book, coupled with all the advice

on preparing and cooking, will reveal the enormous versatility of this truly wonderful fish.

THE KING OF FISH

No fish captures the imagination quite like salmon. Whether it is the romantic vision of a lone fisherman casting his line in a Scottish river on a misty morning, the creature's legendary leap, or its almost mystical migratory habits, salmon inspires a sense of wonder.

The flavour of wild salmon is superb, and although farmed salmon seldom comes close in terms of texture or taste, the cheaper alternative does provide good quality protein to many people who might otherwise be denied the opportunity of trying this delicious fish. Choosing responsibly farmed salmon may also be more environmentally sound in an era when wild Atlantic salmon stocks are falling fast.

HISTORY

There is ample evidence that salmon has been a valuable food source for thousands of years. The Tlingits, who inhabited present-day Alaska some eight thousand years ago, were typical of hunter-gatherer groups living along the east and west coasts of America. For much of the year they caught cod, halibut and herring, along with larger marine mammals, but as the weather

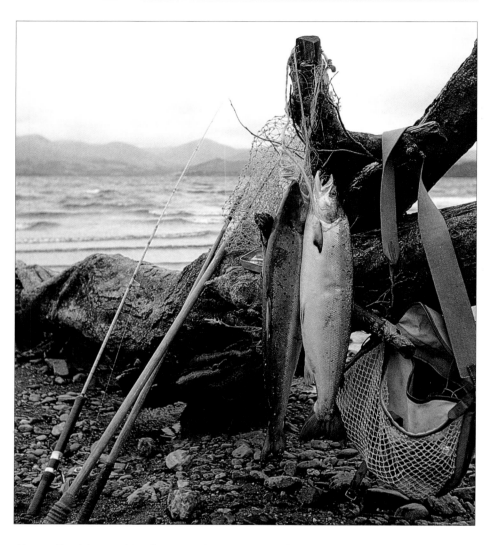

Above: Freshly caught salmon on the shores of Loch Lomond, Scotland.

warmed they moved to their summer camps for one of the most important events of their year: the salmon run. As the fish returned to their native rivers, the hunters trapped them or caught them using primitive hooks and lines. The fish were highly valued as a winter food supply, to supplement the game hunted towards the turn of the year.

Across the Atlantic, salmon was equally highly sought after. Mesolithic fishermen in Ireland are known to have feasted on salmon during the summer months, and to have preserved stocks for winter. In fact, salmon was so highly regarded in Ireland that the fish passed into mythology in tales like the legend of the Salmon of Knowledge.

In Scotland, a country whose name is synonymous with salmon, the importance of the fish was quickly recognized, and William the Lion, who ruled Scotland from 1165 to 1214, introduced legislation to protect salmon.

Two centuries later, in one of the first instances of environmental legislation, the Corporation of Dublin introduced a law forbidding Irish tanners polluting the river Liffey and threatening fish stocks. Salmon are fastidious creatures and will only thrive in pure water.

Throughout the Middle Ages, salmon was a popular food, either braised with spices, potted, salted or made into pies or pastes. In later centuries it became a luxury item, often teamed with other extravagant ingredients, such as lobster. Only recently has salmon once again become affordable.

The Salmon of Knowledge
According to Irish legend, the first person to eat the flesh of the Salmon of Knowledge would be endowed with superhuman intelligence. The fish was a wily creature, almost impossible to capture, but the tale tells how it was eventually landed and cooked by a druid called Finegas. A precocious young fair-haired lad called Fionn MacCumhaill happened by just as the fish was cooked to perfection. Before Finegas could take his first mouthful, Fionn reached out a hand to steal a piece and burnt his thumb in the process. He put his thumb in his mouth to cool it down, and at that moment, all knowledge was his. Fionn became a great hero and his exploits are recounted in dozens of Irish folk tales.

Declining stocks

Wild stocks of Atlantic salmon have reduced by 50 per cent in the last 20 years. In Scotland, wild salmon stocks have fallen by more than 80 per cent in the last three decades. The problem is being remedied to a degree by renewal programmes, which aim to reintroduce wild salmon to Scottish rivers, but recovery will take many years. In the meantime, the Marine Conservation Society recommends that consumers seeking Atlantic salmon purchase responsibly farmed salmon instead.

RANGE AND HABITAT

Salmon are native to the northern hemisphere. Their range naturally extends from the Arctic Circle to the Tropic of Cancer, although they have been introduced into Australia, New Zealand, South America and southern Africa. Classified as Atlantic or Pacific salmon, there are several different varieties. Most are anadromous, which means that they migrate from the sea to fresh waters to spawn. There are some non-migratory species in land-locked lakes in Europe and North America.

LIFE CYCLE

The curious life cycle of the salmon has intrigued fishermen and naturalists for generations. A female Atlantic salmon produces an average of around 1400 eggs per 1kg/2¼lb of body weight. When spawning occurs, in early winter, she will scoop out a shallow depression, known as a redd, in the gravel on the river bed. She does this by turning on to her side and flexing and relaxing her body, creating a current that is capable of moving quite large pebbles. When the redd is deep enough, she extrudes some eggs, which are then fertilized by a male salmon. She continues in this way, often making several redds, until all the fertilized eggs have been deposited and covered with gravel.

Right: Fresh sockeyes, a type of Pacific salmon, kept on ice at the fishmongers.

The eggs hatch about four months later. The tiny hatchlings are first called alevins, then parr, and then smolts. They remain in the river of their birth for up to five years, depending on the variety of salmon, food supply and water temperature, until they are sufficiently mature to journey to the deep-sea feeding grounds. Some may return a year later, as grilse, while others travel further and stay away for several years before returning as adult salmon, weighing up to 14kg/31lb.

The homing instinct, which drives salmon to return to the precise spot where they were spawned, is very mysterious. Some scientists believe that a navigational sense similar to that of migratory birds enables salmon to return to the area of their birth, while chemical imprinting acts like a fine-tuning mechanism, making it possible for them to recognize the smell of their home river and even the exact gravel bed where they originally hatched.

Returning home to spawn is considerably more arduous than the outward journey, as the fish must swim upstream. To do so, many perform astonishing leaps, and the sight of salmon negotiating a waterfall in this way is very impressive.

SALMON FARMING

The first salmon hatcheries, where the eggs from female fish were artificially fertilized and incubated, were developed around the middle of the 19th century, but it was not until the 1970s that commercial salmon farms were established, first in Norway and then soon after in Scotland.

Today, commercial salmon farming is big business, but it is not without problems. Although there are plenty of highly responsible fish farmers, raising fish in a manner that mimics as closely as possible conditions in the wild, there are others who employ intensive methods similar to those used in some factory chicken farms. Such agrochemical fish farmers frequently pollute rivers with pesticides, waste fish food and sewage. The salmon are penned in tightly, making them vulnerable to disease and infestation by fish lice. When they escape, as they often do, they infect wild fish. The escapees also breed with wild fish, putting already compromised natural stocks at risk. Consumers can avoid contributing to this problem by making sure that any farmed salmon they buy comes from a farm with a recognized organic certification.

COOKING

Salmon is a very versatile fish. Whether you serve it raw as sushi, brined as gravlax, or cook it in any of the myriad ways described in this book, it is delicious, nourishing, and an excellent source of the omega-3 fatty acids that are so important for a healthy heart.

TYPES OF SALMON

There are several species of this superb fish, identified initially by the names of the northern oceans in which they spend most of their adult lives. Atlantic salmon are generally judged to have the finest flavour, but the various species of Pacific salmon have their admirers too.

ATLANTIC SALMON *(Salmo salar)*

There is only one species of Atlantic salmon. Its Latin name – *salar* – means leaper, and is a tribute to the creature's athleticism as it travels upstream to the spawning grounds. Atlantic salmon are sleek and muscular, with powerful bodies that contrast with their small heads. On their heads and silvery-blue backs are tiny black crosses. Their sides are silver and the bellies are white. It is quite difficult to tell the sex of immature cock and hen salmon, but during the spawning run, cock salmon develop distinctive hooks or kypes on their lower jaws, making it much easier to tell them apart.

The best salmon are those caught at the start of their spawning run, when they are fat and in prime condition. After leaving the sea, they will not feed again until they return from the spawning grounds, so by the time they get back to sea (if they get back; many salmon die after spawning) they are lean and scrawny.

The average Atlantic salmon weighs about 4.5kg/10lb when mature. The flesh of the wild fish is deep pink in colour, and is firm, succulent and full of flavour.

Salmon roe

The roe of salmon is a beautiful orange-pink colour. It does not have the depth of flavour of sturgeon caviar, but is nonetheless delicious with a squeeze of fresh lemon. The eggs are larger than those of sturgeon and have a delicate, mild flavour and excellent texture. Use them to garnish salmon dishes, or try them with blinis and sour cream. The roe is generally sold in jars, sometimes as *keta*, which is the Russian name for chum salmon.

PACIFIC SALMON *(Oncorhynchus)*

There are six species of Pacific salmon. Five are native to North America and the sixth, masu, is found in Japan.

Sockeye salmon *(Oncorhynchus nerka)*

Slender and silvery when at sea, with blue-black shading on their backs, sockeye salmon are very colourful at the spawning stage. Their heads become olive green and their bodies turn bright red. This has earned them the alternative name of red salmon, and they are also known colloquially as bluebacks. The flesh is an intense red, which is not diminished by canning. Rich and flavourful, it has a high fat content. In the canning industry, sockeye salmon has the highest grade. Smaller than some of the other types of Pacific salmon, sockeyes can weigh as much as 7kg/15½lb, but the average fish on sale is around half this size.

Chinook salmon *(Oncorhynchus tschawytscha)*

Also called the king salmon, this is the largest of the Pacific salmon and takes its common name from the native American tribe for whom they were a vital food source. Chunky in appearance, chinook salmon have silvery bodies with dark backs. These sport sizeable black spots, which are also on the tail. When they spawn, cock chinooks become dark red. The colour is particularly noticeable on the tail fin. The tender, soft-textured flesh ranges from off-white to pinkish-red. The average chinook weighs around 7kg/15½lb, but can grow to over 45kg/100lb.

Coho salmon *(Oncorhynchus kisutch)*

Alternative names for this fish are silver salmon or hooknose, the latter being a reference to the tapered kype or hook that develops on the lower jaw of males during the spawning season. At this stage, too, the silvery sides of cock cohos develop a band of red. Both males and females have small, irregular black spots on the back and tail. The flesh of coho salmon is pinkish orange, with firm texture. It is not as fatty as Chinook or sockeye salmon, and is seldom canned. A popular fish for farming, especially in the north-western United States, cohos are marketed at a weight of around 275g/10oz.

Chum salmon *(Oncorhynchus keta)*

At sea, these slim, elongated fish have silver skins with blue-green backs, without the black spots typical of other species. As they near the spawning season, males develop an olive green hue, and red bands appear on their sides. The pale flesh is lower in fat and not as flavourful as some other varieties. Mature chum salmon weigh around 4.5kg/10lb. Also known as keta, they are widely found in Asian waters.

Above: Atlantic salmon steaks (left) and middle cut

Above: Atlantic salmon

Pink salmon *(Oncorhynchus gorbuscha)*

The smallest members of the Pacific salmon family, these have pale silver skins, with large black spots on the back and tail, and smaller scales. During the spawning season, cocks and hens become greenish brown in colour. They have pale pink flesh, which is widely used for canning. The average pink salmon weighs around 1.8kg/4lb.

Masu salmon *(Oncorhynchus masou)*

This type of Pacific salmon is mainly found off the coast of northern Japan. It is a popular game fish, but in recent years stocks have dwindled due to environmental degradation of the rivers where the fish spawn. The flesh of masu salmon is of excellent quality and this, together with the rarity value, makes it an expensive buy.

Nutrition

Salmon is a valuable protein food. It is rich in omega-3 fatty acids, which lower blood triglycerides and cholesterol levels, keeping the heart healthy, and is a good source of Vitamin A and the B-group vitamins. Farmed salmon is fatter than wild salmon, and delivers more omega-3. Smoked salmon is less nutritious, as the smoking process introduces salt and reduces nutrient levels.

CANNED SALMON

This tastes nothing like fresh salmon, and has a different texture, but it is a richer source of calcium because the bones soften during the canning process and can be eaten. Several grades are available, from the cheapest pink salmon to the best quality wild red Alaskan fish. The latter has a better flavour and texture, but pink salmon delivers higher omega-3 values. Use for mousses, quiches and fish cakes.

SMOKED SALMON

The best smoked salmon tastes so good that it would be easy to dedicate an entire cookbook to it. Smoked salmon is made by brining the fish, then dry curing it in sugar with flavourings such as whisky or molasses, and smoking it over oak or other wood chips. Cold smoking involves curing the salmon at a temperature of less than 33°C/91°F and does not actually cook the fish. For hot smoking, the temperature is 70–80°C/158–176°F and the fish is smoked and cooked simultaneously.

Depending on the strength of the cure, the type of wood chip used and the smoking time, the colour can be anything from pale pink to deep red. The quality of smoked salmon varies enormously. Avoid very cheap smoked salmon as it is likely to be thickly cut and so heavily smoked that the delicate flavour is all but overwhelmed. Good smoked salmon should always be moist and succulent.

Right: Smoked salmon

Buying *and* Storing Salmon

When buying salmon, whether you are choosing a whole fish for a special celebration or just buying steaks for a family supper, it pays to buy from a reputable supplier who knows his product. It is surprising how many fishmongers say they don't like fish. If that's the case, shop elsewhere, for an enthusiast is far more likely to take care when buying his fish. The ideal supplier receives daily deliveries of fish, which are kept cold on a bed of regularly replenished crushed ice or in a refrigerated cabinet. Supermarkets can be a good source of salmon. Most develop good relationships with their own suppliers, and are well aware of how important it is to have well trained, helpful staff to advise their customers.

BUYING WHOLE SALMON

Look for a fish that has shiny skin and scales that are firmly attached. The skin should feel cold and firm, and should spring back when lightly pressed. If the indentation remains, the fish is not perfectly fresh. The eyes should be clear and slightly bulbous. Cloudy or sunken eyes are a sign that the fish has been badly handled or is old. The gills should always be bright pink, not a dull brown.

Smell can also be a good indication of freshness. There should be barely any odour except perhaps the faintest aroma of riverweed.

Serving a whole salmon is inevitably a treat, so it makes sense to buy the best you can afford. Wild salmon will be considerably more expensive than farmed, but the taste will be its own reward. Order the fish in good time from your supplier, so that he can obtain it on the day required. Given notice, a good fishmonger will gut, clean and scale the fish, and will also fillet it, if that is what you want. Ask him for the trimmings, as these can be used to make fish stock.

BUYING PORTIONS

Salmon steaks, fillets or cutlets are a good buy. Salmon portions take little time to cook and can be prepared in many different ways, whether steamed, grilled (broiled), fried or baked. One of the most delicious ways of cooking salmon steaks is on a ridged grill (broiling) pan or griddle, with a little butter and oil, a dash of Tabasco and a squeeze of fresh lemon juice. As with whole salmon, buy portions on the

Below: Salmon steaks

day you plan to cook them. Although fish can be kept chilled for up to two days before being eaten, valuable nutrients will be lost if it is left to languish in the refrigerator.

SUSHI

If you are buying salmon to use raw in sushi or sashimi, the advice given about freshness is doubly important. It is vital that you can rely on your supplier to obtain the best possible fish, and for that reason it is better to order the fish in advance. Ask for a chunk from a large salmon, rather than ready-cut steaks. In Japan, fresh salmon is not used for sushi because of the risk of parasite infestation. Smoked salmon is sometimes used instead.

QUANTITIES

Allow about 175g/6oz fish fillet, cutlets or steaks for serving as a main course. There is a lot of wastage on a whole fish, so allow at least 300g/11oz per person when buying fish in this way.

STORING

It is a good idea to put salmon straight into a chiller bag when you buy it, and transfer it to the coldest part of your refrigerator as soon as you get home. If you have a meat keeper, use that for storage, but make sure that the salmon is very well wrapped, so it does not taint anything else in the refrigerator.

FREEZING

Salmon tastes best fresh, but it is sometimes not practical to cook it straight away. In that case, it is better to freeze it. Unlike some more delicate fish, salmon freezes quite well, retaining much of the original texture and taste. If you buy salmon ready-frozen, make sure it comes from a reputable supplier with a rapid turnover. Avoid freezing salmon for more than 1 month, and thaw it gradually, overnight in the refrigerator if possible. If defrosting in the microwave, separate pieces as soon as possible without tearing the flesh. Remove from the microwave when still slightly icy; if fish is thawed too much it will start to dry out.

PREPARING SALMON

Many fish suppliers will prepare fresh fish for you on request, but it is not difficult to do at home, given a sharp filleting knife and a little dexterity.

SCALING

If a salmon is going to be cooked whole, and you intend removing the skin before or after cooking it, there is no need to scale it. Scaling is essential if the salmon is to be cut into portions. The supplier will do this for you if you ask him, but if doing the job yourself, remove the fins before you start, as they can be a source of bacteria, and are likely to get in the way when you are descaling the fish. Work in the kitchen sink, to contain the scales, and so that you have access to running water.

1 Wash the whole salmon under cold water. Cut off the three fins on the underbelly, from the head to the tail, then turn the fish over and remove the dorsal fins on the back. Be careful when doing this as fins can be sharp.

2 Using a cloth to hold the fish by the tail, use a fish scaler or the back of a large cook's knife to remove the scales, working from the tail to the head. Rinse the fish and repeat the process as many times as necessary.

GUTTING/CLEANING AND BONING

You may prefer to ask your fish supplier to do this part of the preparation for you because it is a messy job. If you are doing it yourself, work on a stable work surface, and rest the fish on several thicknesses of newspaper topped with a large sheet of greaseproof (waxed) paper. Always make sure you dispose of the fish innards by wrapping them securely and removing them to an outside bin.

If you intend to serve the salmon whole, with the head on, you will need to clean it through the gills. This is slightly trickier than cleaning it by slicing through the belly, but it will preserve the appearance of the fish.

Whichever method of cleaning you choose, it is important to completely remove the gills, which would give an unpleasant, bitter taste if left on. Do this by lifting up the gill flaps, which are located on either side of the head of the fish. Push out the frilly gills and use a sharp knife to cut them off at the back of the head, under the jawbone.

Whether you are planning to cook a whole fish or to divide it into separate pieces, it will then be necessary to remove the backbone and pin bones.

Cleaning through the belly

Make sure you have your work surface well covered before you start. Use a sharp, sturdy knife, such as a filleting knife, which will allow you to make firm, smooth cuts through the fish.

1 Starting at the site of the anal fin at the tail end of the salmon, slit open the belly from tail to head, using a short, sharp filleting knife. Try to work with one clean stroke, rather than several jagged movements.

2 Carefully pull out the salmon innards, severing them at the throat and tail if necessary. Remove the gills and use a knife to scrape out the cavity, removing any blood vessels adjacent to the backbone. If left, these could impart a bitter taste when the salmon is cooked. Wash the cavity carefully with cold running water, then carefully pat the salmon dry with kitchen paper. Double wrap the innards, then put them in a sealed plastic bag in the outside bin.

Essential equipment

If you plan to prepare your own whole fish at home, it is important to make sure you that have all the necessary tools to hand. Cleaning, boning and filleting fish is relatively straightforward once you know the necessary techniques, but trying to do it without the right equipment will make your task more difficult. Fortunately, these are not unusual or expensive items.

Fish scaler The best way to remove scales from salmon skin is with a fish scaler. Brushing the back and sides of the fish with this handy utensil will get rid of scales quickly and easily.

Chef's knife A large heavy knife is invaluable for cutting whole salmon into steaks and cutlets.

Filleting knife For skinning and filleting salmon, use a flexible, long-bladed knife. Sharpen it before you start work on the fish to make sure it cuts cleanly and evenly through fish skin and flesh.

Kitchen scissors Sharp scissors with serrated edges will make short work of removing fish fins and tails.

Cleaning through the gills

This method preserves the appearance of the fish, and this is important if you plan to serve the fish whole. Make sure you have your work surface well covered before you start. Use a sharp, flexible knife, such as a filleting knife, which will allow you to make firm, smooth cuts through the flesh. Remove the gills after cleaning the fish, otherwise they will give the meat a bitter and unpleasant taste.

1 Lay the salmon on its side. Using scissors or a sharp filleting knife, make an incision in the belly, near the tail end of the fish. Locate the end of the innards with your fingertips, and cut through to separate them from the fish.

2 Using a sharp filleting knife, cut through the bone at the head of the fish, under the lower jaw. Open up the gill flaps, then insert your fingers into the cavity and gently pull out the innards. These should come away through the gill flaps, to leave the belly intact. Remove the gills.

3 Wash the cavity in running water and pat dry with kitchen paper. Double wrap the innards and put them in a sealed plastic bag in the outside bin.

Boning via the belly

If you intend stuffing the salmon and serving it whole – which is a particularly delicious way to cook salmon on the barbecue – you will need to remove the backbone. This is less difficult than it sounds. The secret is to neatly cut away the flesh so that the bones can be pulled away easily. You will need a razor-sharp filleting knife and a pair of kitchen tweezers, which are necessary to remove the small pin bones.

1 Having cleaned the salmon through the belly, place it belly up. Holding a filleting knife with the blade pointing up, and starting from the tail end, slice between the rib bones and the flesh on one side so that you free the ribs.

2 Turn the knife over and finish the job on this side by sliding the blade down the ribs to the backbone, gradually working the ribs free of the flesh. Repeat on the other side. Using sharp scissors, cut out the backbone so you can remove it with the ribs.

3 Use tweezers to remove any stray pin bones. The best way to locate these tiny bones is to feel carefully along the length of the belly with your fingertips. The cavity is now ready for stuffing.

Boning a salmon steak

Salmon cutlets or bone-in steaks are often cheaper to buy than fillets but the bone can be removed quite easily. This will give a strip of fish that can be cooked as it is or folded back into the steak shape and tied neatly for frying.

1 Insert a sharp, thin-bladed knife into the salmon cutlet at the top of the bone. Cut around the bone, staying as close to it as possible, until you reach the centre of the V-shape of the cutlet. Try to work in one smooth movement.

2 Repeat on the other side of the cutlet to free the bone completely. Gently pull out the bone. Skin the fish if you want to make it more manageable.

3 To keep the steak shape, fold the flesh and tie it neatly with string (twine).

FILLETING SALMON

If you've never filleted a round fish before, salmon is a good one to start with, as its large robust size makes the job relatively easy.

1 If the salmon has been cleaned through the belly, place it on its side and make a diagonal cut around the head, behind the gill flap. If it was cleaned through the gills, this cut may already have been made.

2 Slice through the skin from the gill down the middle of the back, holding the knife flat. Keep the knife on top of the backbone and slice the flesh away from the ribs in one piece, using long even strokes and leaving as little flesh on the ribs as possible. For a salmon cleaned through the gills, you will first need to make a cut from the gills along the middle of the belly.

Filleting fish

One advantage of filleting salmon yourself is that you are left with the head and bones for making your own fish stock. Wash the head thoroughly and remove the gills before using them for stock.

3 When the first fillet, on one side of the fish, has been removed, turn the salmon over and cut away the second fillet in the same way. Remove any pin bones with tweezers. Use the bones and trimmings for fish stock, if you like, but not the bitter gills.

SKINNING A SALMON FILLET

Round fish fillets such as salmon are skinned in exactly the same way as flat fish such as hake and skate.

1 Lay the fillet skin side down with the tail towards you. Dip your fingers in a little salt to stop them slipping and grip the tail. Angle the knife towards the skin.

2 With a sawing action, cut along the length of the fillet from the tail to the head, folding the flesh forwards as you go and keeping the skin taut.

Cutting salmon escalopes

Escalopes (US scallops) are thin pieces of boneless meat or fish, which are sometimes coated in egg and breadcrumbs before being fried. To cut salmon escalopes, skin a salmon fillet, then, holding the fillet down with your hand, use a large knife to cut the piece diagonally into thin slices. The blade should be almost flat. Hold it at enough of an angle to obtain slices about 1cm/½in thick. These will cook very quickly.

PREPARING FILLETS FOR COOKING

Salmon fillets can be cooked whole and flat, rolled and secured with a cocktail stick or cut into cubes.

1 If you are cooking the fillets whole, trim them with a sharp knife, cutting off very thin flaps of fish along the edges.

2 To cube a skinned salmon fillet, cut along the length of the fillet, making strips of the desired width. Then cut each strip across into cubes.

3 To roll a fillet, roll the head end towards the tail and tuck the tail underneath. Secure with a cocktail stick (toothpick).

COOKING SALMON

Despite being quite a substantial, meaty fish, salmon cooks quickly. It can be prepared in a wide number of ways, from poaching to pan-frying, grilling (broiling) to baking and braising. It will emerge from a microwave beautifully moist and full of flavour and can be steamed or smoked with equal success.

Court-bouillon

This stock, which is flavoured with white wine and aromatics, is perfect for poaching salmon. Salt should be added only after cooking the salmon, as it can cause the flesh to stiffen. The recipe makes about 1 litre/ 1³/₄ pints/4 cups.

1 Slice 1 small onion, 2 carrots and the white part of 1 large leek. Put the vegetables in a pan.

2 Add 2 fresh parsley stalks, 2 bay leaves, 2 lemon slices, 300ml/ ¹/₂ pint/1¹/₄ cups dry white wine and 90ml/6 tbsp white wine vinegar. Sprinkle in a few white peppercorns. Add 1 litre/1³/₄ pints/4 cups water. Bring to the boil, lower the heat and simmer for 20 minutes. Strain and leave to cool before using.

Whichever method you choose, it is vital to avoid overcooking salmon. In some circles it is served when the flesh still has a ruby tint, but most people prefer salmon that has just turned opaque. Ideally, the fish should finish cooking on the way to the table, so that when it is touched with the fork, the flesh separates easily into meltingly tender flakes.

It is not possible to give precise timings for cooking salmon, since factors such as the thickness of the fish, the cooking method used and the temperature will all come into play. To ensure that the salmon cooks evenly, remove it from the refrigerator at least 30 minutes before cooking.

Salmon is cooked when its internal temperature is around 63°C/145°F, but rather than employ a meat thermometer, which is quite a specialist piece of kitchen equipment, it is best to use a visual check. Gently insert a small sharp knife into the centre of the fish and part the flesh. It should be no longer translucent and should have begun to ease away from the bone. For large pieces of salmon, it may be simpler to press a fork into the thickest part. If the prongs sink into the flesh, meeting only slight resistance near the bone, the salmon is cooked.

POACHING

This is the classic way of cooking salmon. The fish is cooked gently in either water, fish stock or an aromatic court-bouillon, and this ensures that the maximum flavour is retained.

Whole salmon

Use a fish kettle to poach whole salmon. If you do not have a fish kettle you could try to hire one from a local kitchen store, if they offer this service. It is a good idea to measure the length of your fish kettle before you shop for your fish. There's nothing more irritating than bringing home a salmon only to find it will not fit your kettle. If you are not able to obtain a fish kettle, a whole salmon can be wrapped in foil and cooked in the oven. Use the extra-large foil, sometimes known as turkey foil.

Using a fish kettle

1 Remove the metal insert from the fish kettle and place the salmon on this. Lower the salmon into the kettle. Pour over cold court-bouillon, fish stock or water to cover the fish.

2 Add a few fresh herbs, such as parsley, dill or tarragon. Slices of lemon can be laid on top of the salmon.

3 Cover the fish with buttered baking parchment, place the pan over a medium heat and heat slowly until the water just begins to tremble. Simmer until the flesh is just opaque. If you plan to serve the salmon cold, simmer it for only 5 minutes, then remove the kettle from the heat and set it aside without lifting the lid. By the time the poaching liquid has cooled, the salmon will be perfectly cooked.

Butter sauce for poached fish

Poached fish needs very little enhancement other than a simple sauce that has been made from the poaching liquid itself.

1 Remove the cooked fish from the poaching liquid and keep it hot while you make the sauce.

2 Strain the poaching liquid into a pan and place it over a medium heat. Simmer gently until the liquid has reduced by half.

3 Whisk in some cold diced butter or a little double (heavy) cream to make a smooth, velvety sauce. Season with salt and black papper. Pour the sauce over the fish and serve.

Cooking whole salmon in foil

If you do not have a fish kettle, a whole salmon can be baked in the oven. Have ready a large piece of strong foil. Brush on 15ml/1 tbsp oil. Place the salmon on the foil and tuck some lemon slices inside the cavity. Place more lemon slices on top. Wrap the salmon loosely but securely in the foil and support in a roasting pan. Bake in a preheated oven at 150°C/300°F/Gas 2 for 10–15 minutes per 450g/1lb if under 2.3kg/5lb or 8 minutes per 450g/1lb if over that weight. Check frequently towards the end of cooking as timings will vary, depending on your oven and the thickness of the fish. If the salmon is very large, it may be simpler to cook it in sections, then reassemble it for serving. Clever garnishing can cover any joins.

Salmon portions

A large piece of salmon can be cooked in a pan, following the method for poaching in a fish kettle. Small portions are best poached in a dish that is large enough to hold them in a single layer.

1 Place the salmon portions in a shallow flameproof dish. Pour over court-bouillon, light fish stock or water.

2 Cover the fish with buttered baking parchment. Bring the liquid slowly to simmering point. By this time, thin portions may be cooked. Lower the heat, cover and poach thicker portions for 5–10 minutes more, until opaque.

Using the dishwasher

Many cooks claim that the best way to poach salmon is in the dishwasher. The suggested technique involves wrapping the fish in several layers of foil, placing it on the top shelf of the thoroughly clean machine, and then running the dishwasher through the hottest cycle – without detergent, of course. While this might work if the salmon is relatively small and the dishwasher offers an extra-long hot cycle, a test in a standard dishwasher was unsuccessful. The salmon was beautifully moist, but only the thinnest parts were cooked.

Fish stock

It is easy and economical to make fish stock. For 1 litre/1³/₄ pints/ 4 cups stock you will need about 1kg/2¹/₄lb white fish bones and trimmings from the fishmonger. Do not leave the stock simmering on the stove – after 20 minutes the flavour will deteriorate.

1 Wash any fish heads thoroughly and remove the gills, which would make the stock bitter. Chop the heads and bones if necessary. Put them in a large pan.

2 Slice the white part of 1 leek or ¹/₂ fennel bulb. Chop 1 onion and 1 celery stick. Add to the fish heads and bones in the pan.

3 Pour in 150ml/¹/₄ pint/²/₃ cup dry white wine and 1 litre/1³/₄ pints/ 4 cups water. Add 6 white peppercorns and a bouquet garni. Bring to the boil.

4 Lower the heat and simmer for 20 minutes. Remove from the heat, strain through a sieve lined with muslin (cheesecloth) and cool.

BAKING AND BRAISING

If you want to cook salmon slowly along with other vegetables and flavourings, baking and braising are ideal. To ensure the fish cooks evenly, take it out of the refrigerator 30 minutes before cooking. Aim to undercook the fish as the texture will be dry and it will lose its flavour if it is allowed to cook for too long. You can give it a little extra cooking if necessary.

Baking fillets

Salmon steaks, fillets and cutlets can all be baked in the oven. Check the fish frequently because cooking times will vary, depending on the cut and size of the fish, the method of baking and the effectiveness of your oven.

Chunky salmon steaks and cutlets are perfect for baking in a roasting pan in the oven. The temperature should be no higher than 200°C/400°F/Gas 6. Keep the fish moist by coating it in a sauce or olive oil or by wrapping it in foil.

Another way of retaining maximum moisture is to cook the salmon *en papillote*, which means in a foil or paper parcel. Add a couple of slices of lemon and some fresh dill or other herbs. No additional fat is needed, so this is a very healthy option.

Braising fillets

This is an excellent cooking method for larger salmon fillets. Adding the stock helps to keep the fish beautifully moist.

1 Butter a flameproof dish and arrange a thick bed of thinly sliced or shredded vegetables on the base. A mixture of leeks, fennel and carrots works well.

2 Place the fish on top of the vegetables and pour on enough dry white wine, court-bouillon or light fish stock to come nearly halfway up the fish.

3 Sprinkle over 15ml/1 tbsp chopped fresh herbs, then cover with buttered baking parchment and set over a high heat. Bring the liquid to the boil. Braise over a low heat on top of the stove or in an oven preheated to 180°C/350°F/Gas 4 for 10–15 minutes.

FRYING

Pan-frying is particularly well-suited to salmon because the flesh is robust and the flavours will not be diminished. Stir-frying in a wok is just as tasty, but it uses less oil and makes a healthier alternative to pan-frying.

Pan-frying

Salmon tastes absolutely delicious when lightly pan-fried in butter, fruity olive oil or a mixture of the two.

Heat the fat in the pan. When it is very hot, add the fish and seal briefly on both sides. Lower the heat and cook the fish gently until done. If the pieces of fish are large or the recipe is more complex it may be necessary to finish cooking the fish in an oven preheated to 180°C/350°F/Gas 4.

Searing

This method gives the best results with thick fillets of salmon, with the skin on.

Smear the base of a frying pan or griddle with a little oil and heat until smoking. Brush both sides of the salmon with oil and put into the hot pan, skin down. Sear for 2 minutes, until the skin is golden brown, then turn the fish over and cook the other side.

Stir-frying

This quick Asian cooking style is perfect for many types of fish. Strips of salmon taste delicious stir-fried with thinly sliced spring onions (scallions) and slices of baby fennel. Stir-fry the vegetables briefly in hot oil, then add the salmon strips, lightly moistened with soy sauce, and stir-fry for 1–2 minutes until cooked but still in one piece.

1 Cut the salmon fillets into bitesize strips. Toss in a little cornflour (cornstarch) to prevent them falling apart as they cook in the oil.

2 Heat vegetable oil in a wok or frying pan over a very high heat. Add the pieces of salmon to the wok and stir-fry for a few moments. You may need to cook the pieces in batches, depending on the amount of fish you wish to cook and the size of your wok.

3 As each batch of salmon pieces is cooked, remove them from the wok and keep warm as you cook further batches.

Deep-frying salmon

Salmon pieces are seldom deep-fried in the way that cod or haddock are. The reason for this is not so much because salmon is not suitable for deep-frying – quite the opposite in fact, because its firm, meaty flesh is perfectly capable of holding its shape – but because frying impairs the special flavour and texture. The exception is when thin strips of salmon fillet are transformed into goujons by coating them in milk and flour and deep-frying them in oil.

Goujons of salmon

Crisp on the outside and succulent and tender within, salmon goujons taste wonderful served with a creamy dipping sauce.

SERVES 4

INGREDIENTS
  1 salmon fillet, about 350g/12oz
  120ml/4fl oz/$^1/_2$ cup milk
  50g/2oz/$^1/_2$ cup plain
    (all-purpose) flour
  salt and ground black pepper
  oil, for deep-frying

1 Skin the salmon fillet and cut it into 7.5 x 2.5cm/3 x 1in strips. Pour the milk into a shallow bowl. Season the flour and spread it out in a separate shallow bowl.

2 Dip the salmon strips into the milk, then into the seasoned flour. Shake off the excess flour.

3 Heat the oil for deep-frying to about 185°C/360°F or until a small cube of bread dropped into the oil turns brown in 30 seconds.

4 Lower the salmon strips into the oil, adding four or five at a time. Fry for 3 minutes, turning them occasionally with a slotted spoon, until they have risen to the surface and are golden brown in colour.

5 Lift out each goujon in turn with a slotted spoon and drain on kitchen paper. Keep hot in the oven while you cook successive batches.

ON THE BARBECUE

This is a very good way of cooking salmon. Either marinate steaks or thick fillets (with the skin on) for at least an hour before cooking, or brush them with vegetable or olive oil just before cooking over medium coals. If you are entertaining in large numbers, you could cook a whole salmon on the barbecue. If you have a hinged grill, put the prepared salmon directly on the grill. Otherwise, wrap the salmon in a large sheet of foil. A 2.25kg/5lb salmon will take from 45 minutes to 1 hour to cook, depending on the heat of the coals and whether or not the fish is wrapped in foil.

Marinate the salmon pieces in a mixture of olive oil and lemon juice, making deep slashes in the side of the fish so that the marinade penetrates right the way through and the heat is conducted evenly through the flesh. Leave the fish in the refrigerator to marinate for a minimum of 1 hour.

A ridged griddle set on the barbecue is good for cooking salmon. Grease it lightly with oil to prevent the skin of the salmon from sticking – an oil spray will give the best coverage with the least amount of oil.

GRILLING

When grilling (broiling) salmon steaks or fillets, high heat should be used initially, to seal in the fish juices. Regardless of the recipe, the fish will always benefit from being marinated in a mixture of oil and lemon juice before being grilled. Brush the grill (broiling) rack with oil, and if the fish has not been marinated, brush it with oil too. Turn thick salmon steaks or fillets over once the surface is sealed, and grill the other side until cooked through. Thin fillets will not need to be turned. Cubes of salmon make excellent kebabs.

MICROWAVING

Salmon cooks well in the microwave. Always cover the fish with microwave clear film (plastic wrap). Cook on full power (100 per cent) for the time recommended in your handbook, then give it a resting period so that it finishes cooking by residual heat. As a general guide, thick fillets, steaks and cutlets will take 4–5 minutes and should be left to stand for a further 5 minutes.

Cook salmon fillets in a single layer in a microwave dish. Put thinner parts towards the centre, or tuck a thin end underneath a thicker portion.

ROASTING

Thick pieces of salmon can be roasted successfully. As with grilling it is a good idea to marinate the fish in oil and lemon juice beforehand. Preheat the oven to 230°C/450°F/Gas 8, with the roasting pan inside. Add the pieces of fish, skin side down, to the hot pan. This will sear the skin and help to retain the juices. Fillets will take about 10–12 minutes; steaks 15–20 minutes.

STEAMING

This is the healthiest way of cooking salmon, since no extra fat is required and nutrients are retained, and the steaming process enhances the natural flavour. Salmon cooks quickly this way, but even if you overcook it the fish will retain its shape and remain moist.

1 Half-fill the base pan of a metal steamer with water and bring to the boil. Lower the steamer insert into the base, making sure that it stands well clear of the boiling water.

2 Place the fish in a single layer in the steamer basket, leaving room for the steam to circulate freely. Add fresh herbs with the salmon if you like.

3 Lay a sheet of greaseproof (waxed) paper loosely over the surface of the fish, then cover the pan tightly with a lid or foil. Steam until the fish is just cooked through.

4 Salmon cooks very quickly in a steamer, but take care that the level of the water does not fall too low, or the base of the pan will burn. Check once or twice during cooking and keep a kettle of boiling water on hand to top it up if necessary.

Alternative steaming methods

There are plenty of purpose-made steamers on the market, ranging from the hugely expensive stainless steel models to modest Chinese bamboo baskets. However, you can easily improvise with a large pan, any perforated container, such as a colander or sieve, and some foil. It is important to make sure that the pan is large enough to hold several inches of water.

Whatever the type of steamer you use, remember that the golden rule of steaming is not to allow the boiling liquid to touch the steamer basket or the salmon inside it. This would mean that the fish was boiling in water, and all of its nutritional value would be lost.

A Chinese bamboo steamer is ideal for steaming salmon. Arrange the fish, skin side up, on a bed of aromatic flavourings, such as lemon slices and fresh herbs, or on finely shredded vegetables. Place the steamer in a wok or on top of a large pan of boiling water and steam until the fish is cooked.

SMOKING

Salmon can be smoked at home, either in a small domestic smoker or a kettle barbecue. Follow the instructions in your handbook. In the kitchen, the Chinese method of tea smoking works well, but it helps if you have an extractor fan to remove excess smoke.

1 Line a wok with foil and sprinkle in 30ml/2 tbsp each of raw long grain rice, sugar and aromatic tea leaves.

2 Place a wire rack on the wok and add the salmon fillets in a single layer.

3 Cover the wok with a lid or more foil and cook over a very high heat until smoke appears. Lower the heat slightly (some smoke should still escape from the wok) and cook for 10–15 minutes more until the fish is done.

RAW SALMON

Very fresh salmon that has been bought from a reliable fishmonger or supplier can also be served raw, as smoked salmon, sushi or sashimi, or brined to make the delectable Scandinavian speciality known as gravlax.

Home-cured gravlax

Although almost every supermarket sells ready-cured gravlax, it is very easy to prepare at home. For eight people you will need 1–1.2kg/2¼–2½lb of absolutely fresh middle-cut salmon that has already been boned and cut lengthways into two fillets.

1 For the curing mix, mix 30ml/2 tbsp coarse sea salt, 30ml/2 tbsp caster (superfine) sugar, 15–30ml/1–2 tbsp crushed black peppercorns and a handful of chopped fresh dill.

2 Lay one salmon fillet skin side down in a non-metallic dish. Cover with a generous layer of the curing mix. Lay the second fillet on top, skin side up, and sprinkle on the remaining mix. Cover with clear film (plastic wrap).

3 Place a wooden board slightly larger than the non-metallic dish on top of the salmon and weigh it down with heavy cans or weights.

4 Leave in the refrigerator for at least 72 hours, turning the salmon every 12 hours and basting it with the juices that have oozed out. To serve, slice on the diagonal, a little thicker than you would for smoked salmon.

Above: Gravlax

Flavourings for salmon

Salmon is a hugely versatile fish and it works well with a range of flavourings. The following can be used to adapt your own recipes or some of those featured in this book.

Companion flavourings Salmon has a natural affinity for fresh-tasting herbs like parsley, chervil and tarragon. Dill, with its aniseed flavour, is a great favourite, and is essential in the Swedish sugar-and-salt-cured dish, gravlax. Citrus flavourings like lemon and lime are obvious choices, but try lemon grass for a more subtle taste, or that little used but delicious herb, sorrel.

Fusion flavours Aromatics like ginger and galangal go well with salmon, as does fresh garlic. Spring onions (scallions), leeks and shallots are also suitable, and are especially good to use in marinades and sauces. Fennel has a similar flavour to dill, the herb that works so well with salmon, so try roasting salmon on a bed of thinly sliced fennel, with the fronds chopped and added to a sauce or used as a garnish.

Nuts It is well known that almonds go well with trout, but you can try them with salmon too. Brown them in butter or use them in a stuffing for whole salmon. Other nuts you could try include hazelnuts, pine nuts, pistachios and macadamias.

A splash of wine Dry white wine is the obvious choice of alcohol for flavouring salmon, and it is often mixed with court-bouillon. The Medierranean aperitif drinks pastis and ouzo are also appropriate, as they have the slightly aniseed flavour that balances the oiliness of the fish. For warmer flavours, try rice wine such as sake or mirin. Ginger wine could also be used, but don't overdo it, as its powerful flavour could be a bit overwhelming. For an alcohol-free cooking medium, use a good homemade court-bouillon or fish stock or coconut milk.

EQUIPMENT

Although it is perfectly possible to prepare and cook fish without special kitchen equipment, there are a few items which make the process much easier. Some, such as the fish kettle, take up quite a lot of storage space; other gadgets, such as the fish scaler, are relatively small, but all will prove invaluable for cooking fish.

KNIVES, SCISSORS AND SCALERS

Chef's knife
A large heavy knife with a 20–25cm/ 8–10in blade is essential for cutting fish steaks.

Filleting knife
For filleting and skinning fish, you will need a sharp knife with a flexible blade, which is at least 15cm/6in long. This type of knife can also be used for opening shellfish. It is essential to keep a filleting knife razor sharp.

Kitchen scissors
A sturdy, sharp pair of scissors that have a serrated edge are needed for cutting off fins and trimming tails.

Fish scaler
Resembling a rough grater, a fish scaler makes short work of a task that few relish.

PANS

Fish kettle
Long and deep, with rounded edges, this has handles at either end, and a tightly-fitting lid. Inside is a perforated rack or grid on which to lay the fish. This, too, has handles, and enables the cook to lift out the fish flat. Most modern fish kettles are made of stainless steel, but they also come in aluminium,

enamelled steel and copper with a tin-plated interior. Fish kettles are used on the hob (stove top) and are invaluable for cooking whole large fish, such as salmon. Fish kettles can also be used for steaming other foods.

Oval frying pan
Such a simple idea, but intensely practical, this large pan enables you to pan-fry whole fish flat instead of bending them to fit a round pan, spoiling their shape.

Griddle pan
A ribbed cast-iron griddle pan is ideal for searing and grilling fish. They can be round, oval or rectangular. Some of the large griddles need to be used over two electric rings or gas burners on top of a stove.

Steamer
If you steam food frequently, a stainless steel steamer is a good investment. They have a lidded, deep outer pan and a perforated

inner basket. Choose a model with the widest basket you can find. Chinese bamboo steaming baskets are an economical alternative. They come in a variety of sizes, from very small dim sum baskets to very wide baskets that are about 35cm/14in across. Chinese steaming baskets can be stacked one on top of each other so that several layers of food can be cooked at one time. Cheapest of all is a small, collapsible, perforated steamer, which unfolds like a flower to fit any pan.

Below: Stainless steel steamer

Below: Chef's knife

Below: Filleting knife

Below: Scissors

Left: Chinese bamboo steamer

Above: Fish kettle

Left: Fish scalers

Below: Griddle pan

Above: Double hinged grilling rack

Right: Barbecue grilling rack

Below: Tweezers and pins

Wok
A 35cm/14in wok with a lid will be large enough to cope with most types of fish and will prove invaluable in the kitchen. There's no need to reserve this piece of equipment for stir-frying; a wok also makes an effective steamer and can also be used for deep-frying.

SPECIALIST ITEMS

Barbecue grilling racks
A hinged rack in the shape of a fish makes cooking – and turning – a single large fish relatively easy. Also very useful for general purposes is a double-sided hinged grill rack.

These can be square or rectangular and have long handles so that several salmon steaks can be grilled and turned over simultaneously. However, the flat sides do tend to squash the delicate flesh of some fish. Always oil grilling racks before use to prevent the fish from sticking to them.

Fish smoker
The cheapest home-smoker is a lidded metal box with a rack to hold the fish. Smoke produced by placing dampened aromatic oak or other wood chippings, or a sprinkling of fresh herbs, on the coals gives extra flavour to the fish. More convenient (but more expensive) are electric fish smokers. Stove-top models can be used indoors.

OTHER USEFUL UTENSILS

Fish lifter
Resembling an elongated fish slice, the curved and perforated turner is useful for flipping over whole salmon during cooking without breaking them.

Fish slice
A fish slice with a sturdy yet flexible blade will make easy work of turning whole salmon, steaks and cutlets.

Pins
Use dressmaker's pins with round heads to extract tiny pin bones from salmon. For safety's sake, stick them in a cork when not using.

Tweezers
Use these to extract small bones and pin bones from fish fillets.

Above: Wok

Below: Fish lifters

Above: Fish slice

Right: Fish smoker

SOUPS AND APPETIZERS

One of the many attributes of salmon, aside from its excellent flavour and texture, is the delicate pink colour, and nowhere is this capitalized on more effectively than in the preparation of soups and appetizers. Salmon chowder, for instance, looks so delicious in the bowl that it would seem a shame to disturb it, were it not for the wonderful aroma that rises from the surface. Mousses, terrines and pâtés are just as pretty, especially when smoked salmon is used as a wrapper or garnish. The most dramatic effects, however, come from Japanese kitchens, where very fresh raw salmon is enclosed in jet-black yaki-nori to make superb sushi.

CURRIED SALMON SOUP

A hint of mild curry paste really enhances the flavour of this soup, without making it too spicy. Grated creamed coconut adds a luxury touch, while helping to amalgamate the flavours. Served with chunks of warm bread, this makes a substantial appetizer.

SERVES 4

INGREDIENTS
    50g/2oz/¼ cup butter
    2 onions, roughly chopped
    10ml/2 tsp mild curry paste
    475ml/16fl oz/2 cups water
    150ml/¼ pint/⅔ cup white wine
    300ml/½ pint/1¼ cups double
      (heavy) cream
    50g/2oz/½ cup creamed coconut,
      grated or 120ml/4fl oz/½ cup
      coconut cream
    2 potatoes, about 350g/12oz, cubed
    450g/1lb salmon fillet, skinned
      and cut into bitesize pieces
    60ml/4 tbsp chopped fresh
      flat-leaf parsley
  salt and ground black pepper

1 Melt the butter in a large pan, add the onions and cook for about 3–4 minutes until beginning to soften. Stir in the curry paste. Cook for 1 minute more.

2 Add the water, wine, cream and creamed coconut or coconut cream, with seasoning. Bring to the boil, stirring until the coconut has dissolved.

3 Add the potatoes to the pan. Simmer, covered, for about 15 minutes or until they are almost tender. Do not allow them to break down into the mixture.

4 Add the fish gently so as not to break it up. Simmer for 2–3 minutes until just cooked. Add the parsley and adjust the seasoning. Serve immediately.

SALMON CHOWDER

DILL IS THE PERFECT PARTNER FOR SALMON IN THIS CREAMY SOUP FROM THE USA. IT TAKES ITS INSPIRATION FROM THE SATISFYING SOUPS THAT ARE TYPICAL OF THE EASTERN SEABOARD OF THE UNITED STATES AND IS BEST SERVED IMMEDIATELY AFTER COOKING, WHEN THE SALMON IS JUST TENDER.

SERVES 4

INGREDIENTS
  20g/¾oz/1½ tbsp butter
  1 onion, finely chopped
  1 leek, finely chopped
  1 small fennel bulb, finely chopped
  25g/1oz/¼ cup plain
    (all-purpose) flour
  1.75 litres/3 pints/7 cups fish stock
  2 medium potatoes, cut in
    1cm/½in cubes
  450g/1lb salmon fillet, skinned and
    cut into 2cm/¾in cubes
  175ml/6fl oz/¾ cup milk
  120ml/4fl oz/½ cup whipping cream
  30ml/2 tbsp chopped fresh dill
  salt and ground black pepper

1 Melt the butter in a large pan. Add the onion, leek and chopped fennel and cook for 6 minutes until softened.

2 Stir in the flour. Reduce the heat to low and cook for 3 minutes, stirring occasionally with a wooden spoon.

3 Add the fish stock and potatoes to the mixture in the pan. Season with a little salt and ground black pepper. Bring to the boil, then reduce the heat, cover and simmer gently for about 20 minutes or until the potatoes are tender when tested with a fork.

4 Add the cubed salmon fillet and simmer gently for 3–5 minutes until it is just cooked.

5 Stir the milk, cream, and chopped dill into the contents of the pan. Cook until just warmed through, stirring occasionally, but do not allow to boil. Adjust the seasoning to taste, then ladle into warmed soup bowls to serve.

SALMON SOUP WITH SALSA AND ROUILLE

THIS SMART FISH SOUP IS THE PERFECT CHOICE FOR SUMMER ENTERTAINING. SORREL IS A GOOD PARTNER FOR SALMON, BUT DILL OR FENNEL ARE EQUALLY DELICIOUS ALTERNATIVES.

SERVES 4

INGREDIENTS
    90ml/6 tbsp olive oil
    1 onion, chopped
    1 leek, chopped
    1 celery stick, chopped
    1 fennel bulb, roughly chopped
    1 red (bell) pepper, seeded
      and sliced
    3 garlic cloves, chopped
    grated rind and juice of 2 oranges
    1 bay leaf
    400g/14oz can chopped tomatoes
    1.2 litres/2 pints/5 cups fish stock
    pinch of cayenne pepper
    800g/1¾lb salmon fillet, skinned
    300ml/½ pint/1¼ cups double
      (heavy) cream
    salt and ground black pepper
    4 thin slices baguette, to serve

For the ruby salsa
    2 tomatoes, peeled, seeded
      and diced
    ½ small red onion, very finely
      chopped
    15ml/1 tbsp cod's roe
    15ml/1 tbsp chopped fresh sorrel

For the rouille
    120ml/4fl oz/½ cup mayonnaise
    1 garlic clove, crushed
    5ml/1 tsp sun-dried tomato paste

1 Heat the oil in a large pan and add the chopped onion, leek, celery, fennel, pepper and garlic. Cover the pan and cook gently for 20 minutes or until all the vegetables have softened. Do not allow the onion and garlic to brown.

2 Add the orange rind and juice, bay leaf and tomatoes. Cover and cook for 4–5 minutes, stirring occasionally. Add the stock and cayenne, cover the pan and simmer for 30 minutes.

3 Add the salmon and cook gently for 8–10 minutes, until just cooked. Using a slotted spoon, remove the salmon and place it on a large plate.

4 Flake the salmon into large pieces, and remove any bones that were missed when the fish was originally filleted. Put the flaked salmon in a dish and set it aside.

5 Meanwhile, make the salsa. Put the diced tomatoes in a bowl and add the finely chopped red onion. Stir in the cod's roe and the chopped fresh sorrel. Transfer the mixture to a serving dish and set it aside.

6 To make the rouille to top the toast, mix the mayonnaise with the crushed garlic and the sun-dried tomato paste in a bowl.

7 Leave the soup to cool slightly, then remove and discard the bay leaf. Purée the soup in a food processor or blender until smooth, then press it through a fine sieve into the rinsed-out pan.

8 Stir in the cream and season well, then add the flaked salmon. Toast the baguette slices under a hot grill (broiler) on both sides and set aside.

9 Reheat the soup gently without letting it boil. Ladle it into bowls and float the toasted baguette slices on top. Add a spoonful of rouille to each slice of baguette and spoon some ruby salsa on top. Serve immediately.

COOK'S TIP
For a smart presentation, choose wide, shallow soup plates, so that there is plenty of room for the rouille-topped toast to be accommodated on top of the pieces of flaked salmon. The ruby salsa adds the finishing touch.

CUCUMBER AND YOGURT SOUP WITH SALSA

CHARRED SALMON BRINGS A HINT OF HEAT TO THE REFRESHING FLAVOURS OF THIS CHILLED SOUP.
GOOD-LOOKING AND BEAUTIFULLY LIGHT, IT MAKES THE PERFECT OPENER FOR AN AL-FRESCO MEAL.

SERVES 4

INGREDIENTS

3 medium cucumbers
300ml/½ pint/1¼ cups Greek
  (US strained plain) yogurt
250ml/8fl oz/1 cup vegetable stock,
  chilled
120ml/4fl oz/½ cup crème fraîche
15ml/1 tbsp chopped fresh chervil
15ml/1 tbsp chopped fresh chives
15ml/1 tbsp chopped fresh flat-leaf
  parsley
1 small fresh red chilli, seeded and
  very finely chopped
a little oil, for brushing
225g/8oz salmon fillet, skinned and
  cut into eight thin slices
salt and ground black pepper
fresh chervil or chives, to garnish

4 Brush a griddle or frying pan with oil and heat until very hot. Add the salmon slices and sear them for 1–2 minutes, then turn over carefully and sear the other side until tender and charred.

5 Ladle the chilled soup into soup bowls. Top each portion with two slices of salmon, then pile a portion of salsa into the centre. Garnish with the chervil or chives and serve.

1 Peel two of the cucumbers and halve them lengthways. Scoop out and discard the seeds, then roughly chop the flesh. Purée the chopped flesh in a food processor or blender.

2 Add the yogurt, stock, crème fraîche, chervil, chives and seasoning, and process until smooth. Pour into a bowl, cover and chill.

3 Peel, halve and seed the remaining cucumber. Cut the flesh into small neat dice. Mix with the chopped parsley and chilli in a bowl. Cover the salsa and chill until required.

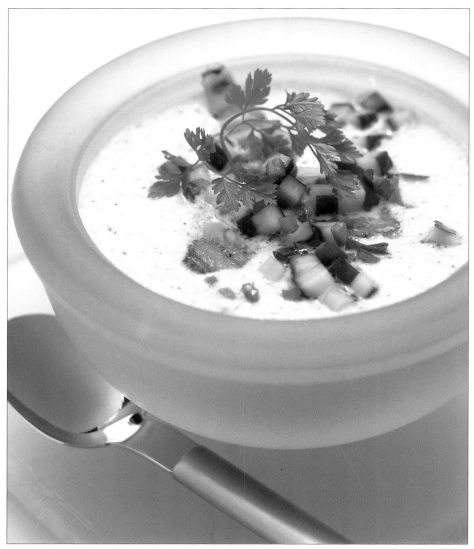

NOODLE, PAK CHOI AND SALMON RAMEN

THIS LIGHTLY SPICED JAPANESE NOODLE SOUP IS ENHANCED BY SLICES OF SEARED FRESH SALMON AND CRISP VEGETABLES. THE CONTRASTS IN TEXTURE ARE AS APPEALING AS THE DELICIOUS TASTE.

SERVES 4

INGREDIENTS
1.5 litres/2½ pints/6 cups good
vegetable stock
2.5cm/1in piece fresh root ginger,
finely sliced
2 garlic cloves, crushed
6 spring onions (scallions), sliced
45ml/3 tbsp soy sauce
45ml/3 tbsp sake
450g/1lb salmon fillet, skinned
5ml/1 tsp groundnut (peanut) oil
350g/12oz ramen or udon noodles
4 small heads pak choi (bok choy),
broken into leaves
1 fresh red chilli, seeded and sliced
50g/2oz/1 cup beansprouts
salt and ground black pepper

1 Pour the stock into a large pan and add the ginger, garlic, and a third of the spring onions.

2 Add the soy sauce and sake. Bring to the boil, then reduce the heat and simmer for 30 minutes.

3 Meanwhile, remove any pin bones from the salmon using tweezers, then cut the salmon on the slant into 12 slices, using a very sharp knife.

4 Brush a ridged griddle or frying pan with the oil and heat until very hot. Sear the salmon slices for 1–2 minutes on each side until tender and marked by the ridges of the pan. Set aside.

COOK'S TIP
To obtain the distinctive stripes on the slices of salmon, it is important that the ridged pan or griddle is very hot before they are added. Avoid moving the slices, or the stripes will become blurred.

5 Cook the ramen or udon noodles in a large pan of boiling water for 4–5 minutes or according to the instructions on the packet. Tip into a colander, drain well and refresh under cold running water. Drain again and set aside.

6 Strain the broth into a clean pan and season, then bring to the boil. Add the pak choi. Using a fork, twist the noodles into four nests and put these into deep bowls. Divide the salmon slices, spring onions, chilli and beansprouts among the bowls. Ladle in the broth.

GRAVLAX

BE GENEROUS WITH THE DILL IN THIS SCANDINAVIAN SPECIALITY — IT ADDS A LOVELY FLAVOUR.

SERVES 12

INGREDIENTS
   1.2kg/2½lb salmon, cleaned and
      with head, tail and bones removed
   45ml/3 tbsp coarse sea salt
   30ml/2 tbsp caster (superfine)
      sugar
   12 black peppercorns, crushed
   large bunch of fresh dill, chopped

For the mustard sauce
   2 egg yolks
   30ml/2 tbsp white wine vinegar
   45ml/3 tbsp mild mustard
   50g/2oz soft light brown sugar
   300ml/½ pint/1¼ cups light olive oil
   30ml/2 tbsp chopped fresh dill
   salt and ground white pepper

1 Place one fillet skin-side down in a non-metallic dish. Sprinkle over the salt, sugar and peppercorns. Cover with half the dill.

2 Lay the other fillet on top and cover with the remaining dill. Set a heavy weight on top of the fish. Cover and chill in the refrigerator for at least 72 hours, turning the salmon every 12 hours and basting it with the brine solution that collects in the dish.

3 Put the egg yolks and half the vinegar and mustard into a food processor. Add the brown sugar and a little salt and white pepper. Process until smooth.

4 With the motor running, gradually add the oil in a steady stream through the feeder tube, continuing to process the mixture until it thickens. Stir in the remaining vinegar and mustard with the dill, then scrape the sauce into a bowl and set it aside.

5 Drain the liquid from the salmon and scrape off any remaining salt. Pat the fish dry. Cut on the diagonal into thin slices and serve with the mustard sauce.

CHILLI ᴬᴺᴰ SALT-CURED SALMON

BUY VERY FRESH FISH FROM A REPUTABLE SOURCE FOR THIS DELICIOUS ALTERNATIVE TO SMOKED SALMON.

SERVES 10

INGREDIENTS
  50g/2oz/¼ cup sea salt
  45ml/3 tbsp caster (superfine) sugar
  5ml/1 tsp chilli powder
  5ml/1 tsp ground black pepper
  45ml/3 tbsp chopped fresh
    coriander (cilantro)
  2 salmon fillets, about 250g/
    9oz each
  fresh flat leaf parsley, to garnish
  garlic mayonnaise, to serve

1 In a bowl, mix together the salt, sugar, chilli powder, pepper and coriander. Rub the mixture into the salmon flesh.

2 Place one of the fillets, skin side down, in a shallow glass dish. Place the other fillet on top, with the skin side up. Cover with foil, then place a weight on top.

3 Chill for 48 hours, turning the fish every 8 hours or so and basting it with the liquid that forms in the dish.

4 Drain the salmon well and transfer to a board. Using a sharp knife, slice it diagonally into wafer-thin slices. Arrange on plates and garnish with sprigs of parsley. Serve with garlic mayonnaise.

COOK'S TIP
For a garnish for the salt-cured salmon, scrape any remaining fish off the skin. Cut the skin into 1cm/½in wide strips and fry for 1 minute in hot oil until crisp. Drain and cool on kitchen paper.

SALMON WITH CUCUMBER SAUCE

CUCUMBER AND FRESH DILL ARE A PERFECT COMBINATION IN THIS UNUSUAL HOT SAUCE, WHICH REALLY COMPLEMENTS THE BAKED SALMON.

SERVES 6–8

INGREDIENTS
1.8kg/4lb salmon, cleaned
  and scaled
melted butter, for brushing
3 fresh parsley or thyme sprigs
½ lemon, halved
orange slices and salad leaves,
  to serve

For the cucumber sauce
1 large cucumber, peeled
25g/1oz/2 tbsp butter
120ml/4fl oz/½ cup dry white wine
45ml/3 tbsp finely chopped
  fresh dill
60ml/4 tbsp sour cream
salt and ground black pepper

3 Meanwhile, halve the cucumber lengthways, scoop out the seeds, then dice the flesh.

4 Place the cucumber in a colander, toss lightly with salt and leave for about 30 minutes to drain. Rinse well, drain again and pat dry.

5 Heat the butter in a small pan, add the cucumber and cook for 2 minutes until translucent. Add the wine and boil briskly until the cucumber is dry. Stir in the dill and sour cream and season to taste. Fillet the salmon and serve with the cucumber sauce, orange slices and salad leaves.

1 Season the salmon. Brush it inside and out with melted butter. Place the herb sprigs and lemon in the cavity.

2 Wrap the salmon in foil, folding the edges together securely, then bake in a preheated oven at 220°C/425°F/Gas 7 for 15 minutes. Remove the fish from the oven and leave in the foil for 1 hour, then remove the skin from the salmon.

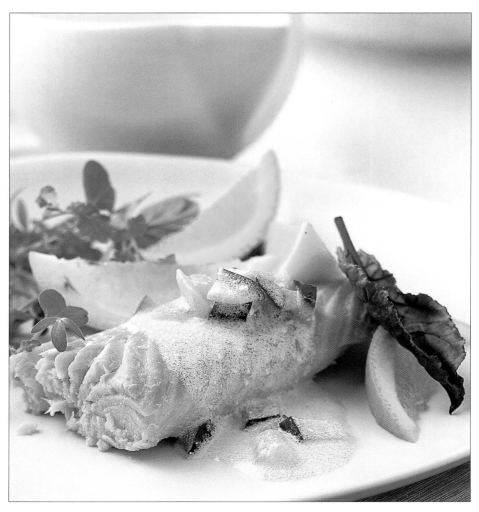

SIMPLE ROLLED SUSHI

SALMON MAKES A SUPERB FILLING FOR THESE SIMPLE ROLLS. ALSO KNOWN AS HOSO-MAKI, THEY MAKE EXCELLENT CANAPÉS. YOU WILL NEED A BAMBOO MAT FOR THE ROLLING PROCESS.

MAKES 12 ROLLS OR 72 SLICES

INGREDIENTS
   400g/14oz/2 cups Japanese short
      grain rice, soaked for 20 minutes
      in water to cover
   550ml/18fl oz/2¼ cups cold water
   55ml/3½ tbsp rice vinegar
   15ml/1 tbsp sugar
   10ml/2 tsp salt
   6 sheets yaki-nori
   200g/7oz very fresh salmon fillet
   200g/7oz very fresh tuna, in
      one piece
   wasabi paste
   ½ cucumber, quartered lengthways
      and seeded
   salmon roe and pickled ginger,
      to garnish (optional)
   shoyu (Japanese soy sauce), to serve

1 Drain the rice, then put it in a pan with the measured water. Bring to the boil, then lower the heat, cover and simmer for 20 minutes, or until all the liquid has been absorbed. Meanwhile, heat the vinegar, sugar and salt in a pan, stir well and cool. Fold into the hot rice, then remove the pan from the heat, cover and leave to stand for 20 minutes.

2 Cut the yaki-nori sheets in half. Cut the salmon and tuna into sticks the length of the long side of the yaki-nori and 1cm/½in square if viewed end-on.

3 Place a sheet of yaki-nori, shiny side down, on a bamboo mat. Divide the rice into 12 portions. Spread one portion over the yaki-nori, leaving a 1cm/½in clear space around the edges.

4 Spread a little wasabi paste in a horizontal line along the middle of the rice and lay one or two sticks of tuna lengthways on this, so that when rolled, the tuna will form a filling.

5 Holding the mat and the edge of the yaki-nori nearest to you, roll up the yaki-nori and rice into a cylinder with the tuna in the middle. Use the mat as a guide – do not roll it into the food. Roll the rice tightly so that it sticks together.

6 Carefully roll the sushi off the mat. Make 11 more rolls in the same way, four for each filling ingredient, but do not use wasabi with the cucumber. Use a wet knife to cut each roll into six slices and stand them on a platter. Garnish the sushi with salmon roe and pickled ginger, if you wish, and serve with shoyu.

RICE IN GREEN TEA WITH SALMON

THIS IS A COMMON JAPANESE SNACK TO HAVE AFTER DRINKS AND NIBBLES. IN THE KYOTO REGION, OFFERING THIS DISH TO GUESTS USED TO BE A POLITE WAY OF SAYING THE PARTY WAS OVER. THE GUESTS WERE EXPECTED TO DECLINE THE OFFER AND LEAVE IMMEDIATELY.

SERVES 4

INGREDIENTS
    150g/5oz salmon fillet
    ¼ sheet nori
    250g/9oz/1¼ cups Japanese short
        grain rice cooked as advised on
        the packet, using 350ml/12fl oz/
        1½ cups water
    15ml/1 tbsp sencha leaves
    600ml/1 pint/2½ cups water
    5ml/1 tsp wasabi paste or 5ml/1 tsp
        wasabi powder mixed with 1.5ml/
        ¼ tsp water (optional)
    20ml/4 tsp shoyu (Japanese soy sauce)
    sea salt

1 Place the salmon fillet in a bowl and cover it with salt. If the fillet is thicker than 2.5cm/1in, slice it in half and salt both halves. Leave for 30 minutes

2 Wipe the salt off the salmon with kitchen paper and grill (broil) the fish under a preheated grill (broiler) for about 5 minutes until cooked through.

3 Using scissors, cut the nori into short, narrow strips about 20 x 5mm/ ¾ x ¼in long, or leave as long narrow strips, if you prefer.

4 Remove the skin and any bones from the salmon, then flake the fish.

5 If the cooked rice is warm, put equal amounts into individual rice bowls or soup bowls. If the rice is cold, put it in a sieve and pour hot water from a kettle over it to warm it up. Drain and pour into the bowls. Place the salmon pieces on top of the rice.

6 Put the sencha leaves in a teapot. Bring the water to the boil, remove from the heat and leave to cool slightly. Pour into the teapot and wait for 45 seconds.

7 Strain the tea gently and evenly over the top of the rice and salmon. Add some nori and wasabi, if using, to the top of each portion of rice, then trickle shoyu over and serve.

COOK'S TIP
Sencha are fine green tea leaves available from Japanese food stores and shops or markets selling specialist teas.

CEVICHE

THIS IS A FRUITY FIRST COURSE OF MARINATED FRESH FISH. TAKE CARE IN CHOOSING THE FISH FOR THIS DISH; IT MUST BE AS FRESH AS POSSIBLE AND SERVED ON THE DAY IT IS MADE, SINCE IT IS "COOKED" BY THE ACTION OF THE CITRUS JUICES, RATHER THAN A MORE CONVENTIONAL METHOD.

SERVES 6

INGREDIENTS

  350g/12oz medium cooked
    prawns (shrimp)
  350g/12oz scallops, removed from
    their shells, with corals intact
  175g/6oz tomatoes
  1 mango, about 175g/6oz
  1 red onion, finely chopped
  350g/12oz salmon fillet
  1 fresh red chilli, seeded and chopped
  12 limes
  30ml/2 tbsp caster (superfine) sugar
  2 pink grapefruit
  3 oranges
  salt and ground black pepper

1 Set aside two prawns for the garnish. Peel the remaining prawns and cut the scallops into 1.2cm/¹/₂in dice.

2 Dice the tomatoes and place in a bowl. Peel the mango, dice the flesh and add it to the bowl with the red onion. Mix well.

3 Skin the salmon, then remove any pin bones with a pair of tweezers. Cut the fish into small pieces and mix with the tomato, mango and onion. Add the chilli and mix well.

4 Squeeze the juice from eight of the limes and add it to the tomato mixture, with the sugar and a little salt and pepper. Stir, cover and leave to marinate in a cool place for 3 hours.

5 Segment the grapefruit, oranges and remaining limes. Drain off as much excess lime juice as possible and mix the fruit segments into the marinated ingredients. Season to taste and serve, garnished with the reserved prawns.

COOK'S TIP
Skinning the salmon fillet will be much easier if you place the fish in the freezer for about 10 minutes first. Cut down to the skin at the narrow end of the fillet, then, holding that end firmly with your free hand, turn the blade and slice the flesh off the skin.

SMOKED SALMON PÂTÉ

THIS LOOKS SOPHISTICATED, BUT IS SURPRISINGLY SIMPLE TO MAKE. THE SMOKED SALMON JACKET
ENCLOSES A MOUTHWATERING SALMON PÂTÉ.

2 Put the remaining smoked salmon into a food processor and add the cream, lemon rind and three-quarters of the lemon juice. Process until smooth, then taste and add more salt and ground black pepper. If the salmon was quite oily, it may also be necessary to add a little more lemon juice.

3 Pack the lined ramekins with the smoked salmon pâté. Bring over the loose strips of salmon to cover the pâté completely. Cover and chill for at least 30 minutes, then turn out of the moulds, lift off and discard the clear film, and serve with the Melba toast.

COOK'S TIP
Process the salmon in short bursts until it is just smooth. Don't over-process the pâté or it will thicken too much and the texture will be compromised.

VARIATIONS
• Try this with smoked trout, which has a lovely rosy colour and a more delicate flavour than smoked salmon.
• A little horseradish cream makes a good addition to the pate, but don't overdo it, or you won't be able to taste the smoked fish.

SERVES 4

INGREDIENTS
    350g/12oz thinly sliced
      smoked salmon
    150ml/¼ pint/⅔ cup double
      (heavy) cream
    finely grated rind and juice of
      1 lemon
    salt and ground black pepper
    Melba toast, to serve

1 Line four small ramekins with clear film (plastic wrap). Line the dishes with 115g/4oz of the smoked salmon, cut into strips long enough to flop over the edges.

SALMON AND PIKE MOUSSE

WHEN SLICED, THIS LIGHT-TEXTURED RUSSIAN MOUSSE LOAF, PATE IZ SHCHUKI, REVEALS A PRETTY LAYER OF PINK SALMON. FOR A SPECIAL OCCASION, SERVE TOPPED WITH RED SALMON ROE.

SERVES 8

INGREDIENTS

10ml/2 tsp oil
225g/8oz salmon fillet, skinned
600ml/1 pint/2½ cups fish stock
finely grated rind and juice of
½ lemon
900g/2lb pike fillets, skinned
4 egg whites
475ml/16fl oz/2 cups double
(heavy) cream
30ml/2 tbsp chopped fresh dill
salt and ground black pepper
red salmon roe or a fresh dill sprig,
to garnish (optional)

COOK'S TIP

If you have difficulty locating pike,
you can substitute turbot, sea bream
or sole for the pike in this recipe.

1 Preheat the oven to 180°C/350°F/
Gas 4. Brush a 900g/2lb loaf pan with
oil and line with baking parchment.

2 Cut the salmon into 5cm/2in strips.
Pour the stock and lemon juice into a
pan and bring to the boil, then turn off
the heat. Add the salmon strips, cover
and leave for 2 minutes. Remove with
a slotted spoon.

3 Cut the pike into cubes and process
in a food processor or blender until
smooth. Lightly whisk the egg whites
with a fork. With the motor of the food
processor or blender running, slowly
pour in the egg whites, then the cream
through the feeder tube or lid. Finally,
add the lemon rind and dill. Taste the
mixture and add a little salt and pepper
if you think more seasoning is needed.

4 Spoon half of the pike mixture into
the prepared loaf pan. Arrange the
poached salmon strips on top, then
carefully spoon in the remaining pike
mixture.

5 Cover the loaf pan with foil and put in
a roasting pan. Add enough boiling
water to come halfway up the sides of
the loaf pan. Bake for 45–50 minutes,
or until firm.

6 Leave on a wire rack to cool, then
chill for at least 3 hours. Invert on to a
serving plate and remove the lining
paper. Serve the mousse in slices.
Garnish with red salmon roe or a sprig
of fresh dill, if you like. A spoonful of
crème fraîche could also be added.

SMOKED SALMON TERRINE <u>WITH</u> LEMONS

This melt-in-the-mouth smoked salmon terrine makes a spectacular first course for a special dinner. If you want to serve it with wrapped individual lemon halves, as suggested in the method, you will need some muslin and raffia.

SERVES 6

INGREDIENTS
    4 sheets leaf gelatine
    60ml/4 tbsp water
    400g/14oz smoked salmon, sliced
    300g/11oz/scant 1½ cups
      cream cheese
    120ml/4fl oz/½ cup crème fraîche
    30ml/2 tbsp dill mustard
    juice of 1 lime
    2 lemons, to garnish

1 Soak the gelatine in the water in a small bowl until softened. Meanwhile, line a 450g/1lb loaf pan with clear film (plastic wrap). Use some of the smoked salmon to line the pan, laying the slices widthways across the base and up the sides and leaving enough hanging over the edge to fold over the top of the filling.

VARIATION
Powdered gelatine can be used instead of the sheets. Substitute 15ml/1 tbsp powdered gelatine. Sprinkle it over the cold water in a heatproof bowl, then set aside until spongy. Place the bowl over simmering water until the gelatine has liquefied completely before adding it to the terrine mixture.

2 Set aside enough of the remaining smoked salmon to make a middle layer the length of the pan. Chop the rest finely by hand or in a food processor. Take care not to over-process the salmon; it must not form a paste.

3 In a bowl, beat the cream cheese, crème fraiche and dill mustard until well combined. Scrape in the chopped salmon and mix with a rubber spatula or a spoon until well combined.

4 Squeeze out the gelatine and put the sheets in a small, heavy pan. Add the lime juice. Place over a low heat until the gelatine has melted, cool slightly, then stir into the salmon mixture.

5 Spoon half the mixture into the lined pan. Lay the reserved smoked salmon slices on the mixture along the length of the pan, then spoon on the rest of the filling and smooth the top.

6 Tap the pan on the surface to expel any trapped air. Fold over the overhanging salmon slices to cover the top. Cover the whole pan with clear film and place in the refrigerator to chill for at least 4 hours, preferably 6–8 hours.

7 If making the lemon garnish, cut one lemon in half widthways. Wrap each half in a small square of muslin (cheesecloth). Gather the muslin at the end of the lemon and tie with raffia.

8 Cut a small "V" from the side of the other lemon. Repeat at 5mm/¼in intervals. Turn out the terrine, then slice. Garnish with the muslin-wrapped lemons and lemon "leaves".

STRIPED FISH TERRINE

ROSE AND CREAM, THE DELICATE COLOURS OF SALMON AND SOLE GIVE THIS TASTY TERRINE A VERY PRETTY APPEARANCE. SERVE IT COLD OR JUST WARM, WITH A HOLLANDAISE SAUCE IF YOU LIKE.

SERVES 8

INGREDIENTS

15ml/1 tbsp sunflower oil
450g/1lb salmon fillet, skinned
450g/1lb sole fillets, skinned
3 egg whites
105ml/7 tbsp double (heavy) cream
15ml/1 tbsp fresh chives,
  finely chopped
juice of 1 lemon
115g/4oz/scant 1 cup fresh or frozen
  peas, cooked
5ml/1 tsp chopped fresh mint leaves
salt, ground white pepper and freshly
  grated nutmeg
thinly sliced cucumber, salad or land
  cress and chives, to garnish

1 Grease a 1 litre/1¾ pint/4 cup loaf pan or terrine with the oil. Slice the salmon thinly; cut it and the sole into long strips, 2.5cm/1in wide. Preheat the oven to 200°C/400°F/Gas 6.

COOK'S TIPS
• Pop the salmon into the freezer about an hour before slicing it. If it is almost frozen, it will be much easier to slice.
• Lining the base of the terrine with a piece of baking parchment before adding the salmon and sole strips will make it easier to turn out.
• If serving the terrine cold, remove it from the refrigerator at least 15 minutes before serving, as the flavour will be diminished if it is too heavily chilled.

2 Line the terrine neatly with alternate slices of salmon and sole, leaving the ends hanging over the edge. You should be left with about a third of the salmon and half the sole.

3 In a grease-free bowl, beat the egg whites with a pinch of salt until they form soft peaks. Purée the remaining sole in a food processor. Spoon into a mixing bowl, season, then fold in two-thirds of the egg whites, followed by two-thirds of the cream. Put half the mixture into a second bowl; stir in the chives. Add nutmeg to the first bowl.

4 Purée the remaining salmon, scrape it into a bowl and add the lemon juice. Fold in the remaining whites and cream.

5 Purée the peas with the mint. Season the mixture and spread it over the base of the terrine, smoothing the surface with a spatula. Spoon over the sole with chives mixture and spread evenly.

6 Add the salmon mixture, then finish with the sole and nutmeg mixture. Cover with the overhanging fish fillets and make a lid of oiled foil. Stand the terrine in a roasting pan and pour in enough boiling water to come halfway up the sides.

7 Bake for 15–20 minutes, until the top fillets are just cooked and the mousse feels springy. Remove the foil, lay a wire rack over the top of the terrine and invert both rack and terrine on to a lipped baking sheet to catch the cooking juices that drain out. Keep these to make fish stock or soup.

8 Leaving the pan in place, let the terrine stand for about 15 minutes, then turn the terrine by inverting it on to a serving dish and lifting off the pan carefully. Serve warm or lightly chilled, garnished with thinly sliced cucumber, salad or land cress and chives.

SALMON DIP

THIS CREAMY SMOKED SALMON DIP WITH HOT ROSEMARY AND CHILLI POTATO WEDGES AND PEPPER STRIPS CAN BE SERVED AS AN APPETIZER OR AS PART OF A BUFFET LUNCH — A GLASS OF CHILLED SPARKLING WHITE WINE IS THE IDEAL ACCOMPANIMENT. IT ALSO MAKES GOOD PARTY FOOD. HAND IT ROUND WITH TORTILLA CHIPS OR CRUDITÉS WHEN YOUR GUESTS ARRIVE.

SERVES 4

INGREDIENTS
115g/4oz smoked salmon
250g/9oz/generous 1 cup
  mascarpone cheese
60ml/4 tbsp chopped fresh chives
grated rind and juice of 1 lemon
1 red (bell) pepper, seeded and cut
  into strips
1 yellow (bell) pepper, seeded and
  cut into strips
sea salt and ground black pepper

For the potato wedges
675g/1½lb large potatoes,
  scrubbed
60ml/4 tbsp olive oil
30ml/2 tbsp chopped fresh
  rosemary
1 fresh red chilli, seeded and
  finely chopped

1 Preheat the oven to 200°C/400°F/ Gas 6. To make the potato wedges, dry the potatoes thoroughly with kitchen paper, then cut them into thick pieces.

VARIATIONS
To give a more intense chilli flavour, roast the potato wedges in a mixture of 30ml/ 2 tbsp chipotle chilli oil and 30ml/2 tbsp olive oil. Leave the seeds in the chilli for extra heat, if you like. If, on the other hand, you don't like hot, spicy flavours, omit the chilli and substitute a finely chopped sweet red (bell) pepper.

2 Pour the oil into a roasting pan and heat it in the oven for 10 minutes. Add the potato wedges to the hot oil, then sprinkle over the chopped fresh rosemary and the finely chopped chilli.

3 Protecting your hand with an oven glove, shake the pan gently to coat the potatoes in the oil, rosemary and chilli. Season well with sea salt and plenty of black pepper. Bake for 50–60 minutes or until tender, turning occasionally to prevent the wedges from sticking to the roasting pan.

4 Cut the smoked salmon into small pieces, using kitchen scissors or a sharp filleting knife.

COOK'S TIP
Slice the potatoes just before cooking, or the cut sides will discolour. It isn't necessary to peel the potatoes if you scrub them thoroughly.

5 Put the mascarpone cheese, chives and lemon rind in a bowl and mix with a fork until thoroughly blended.

6 Add the lemon juice, a little at a time, mixing constantly, so that the mixture is thinned and given a lemony tang, but does not curdle. A reamer is useful for squeezing the lemon, but watch out for the pips (seeds).

7 Add the salmon pieces to the cheese mixture and season with ground black pepper to taste. Transfer into a serving bowl, cover and chill until required.

8 To serve, arrange the pepper strips and potato wedges around the edge of a large serving platter and place the dip to one side or in the centre.

SALMON TORTILLA CONES

WHETHER YOU'RE SNUGGLING UP ON THE SOFA TO WATCH A LATE NIGHT MOVIE OR CATERING FOR A CROWD, THESE SIMPLE YET SOPHISTICATED WRAPS ARE IRRESISTIBLE.

SERVES 4

INGREDIENTS

115g/4oz/½ cup soft white
  (farmer's) cheese
30ml/2 tbsp roughly chopped
  fresh dill
juice of 1 lemon
1 small red onion
15ml/1 tbsp drained bottled capers
30ml/2 tbsp extra virgin olive oil
30ml/2 tbsp roughly chopped fresh
  flat leaf parsley
115g/4oz smoked salmon
8 small or 4 large wheat
  flour tortillas
salt and ground black pepper
lemon wedges, for squeezing

1 Place the soft cheese in a small bowl and mix in half the chopped dill. Add a little salt and pepper and just a dash of the lemon juice to taste. Reserve the remaining lemon juice in a dish.

2 Finely chop the red onion. Add the onion, capers and olive oil to the lemon juice. Add the chopped flat leaf parsley and the remaining dill and stir gently.

3 Cut the smoked salmon into short, thin strips, and add to the red onion mixture. Toss to mix. Season to taste with plenty of pepper.

4 If using small tortillas, leave them whole, but large ones need to be cut in half. Spread a little of the soft cheese mixture on each piece of tortilla and top with the smoked salmon mixture.

5 Roll up the tortillas into cones and secure with wooden cocktail sticks (toothpicks). Arrange on a serving plate and add some lemon wedges, for squeezing. Serve immediately.

VARIATIONS
Try soft cheese with red pesto, chopped sun-dried tomatoes and smoked salmon, or smoked trout pâté with slices of cucumber.

COOK'S TIP
Look out for tortilla wraps in the supermarket. Thinner than traditional Mexican wheat tortillas, these come in several flavours. The spicy tomato ones would be good for this recipe.

SMOKED SALMON AND SPINACH WRAPS

THE CREAMY TEXTURES OF AVOCADO AND HUMMUS AND THE VIBRANT COLOURS OF RED PEPPER AND BABY SPINACH MAKE THESE DELICIOUS WRAPS A FEAST FOR THE EYES AS WELL AS THE TASTE BUDS!

MAKES 6

INGREDIENTS
    2 red (bell) peppers
    30ml/2 tbsp olive oil
    6 large wheat flour tortillas
    1 avocado
    30ml/2 tbsp lemon juice
    115g/4oz/½ cup hummus
    25g/1oz/3 tbsp pine nuts
    50g/2oz baby spinach leaves
    115g/4oz smoked salmon
    salt and ground black pepper

COOK'S TIP
The peppers can also be charred under the grill (broiler) and the tortillas heated in the microwave.

1 Preheat the oven to 180°C/350°F/ Gas 4. Place the peppers in a roasting pan. Drizzle the olive oil over and season with plenty of salt and black pepper. Bake for 25–30 minutes.

2 Peel the skin off the cooked peppers and discard the core and seeds. Cut the pepper flesh into strips.

3 Place the tortillas on a sheet of foil and seal tightly. Warm in the oven for 10 minutes.

4 Meanwhile, cut the avocado in half, remove the stone (pit) and peel, then slice lengthways. Sprinkle with the lemon juice to prevent the avocado flesh from turning brown.

5 Remove the tortillas from the oven. Spread a quarter of the hummus over each wrap, using a round-bladed knife or slim spatula, then sprinkle the pine nuts evenly over the hummus, but leaving the borders free of nuts.

6 Divide the spinach, salmon and peppers among the topped tortillas, placing them in a line down the centre. Roll up each wrap and serve immediately, while still warm. Offer lemon wedges for squeezing, if you like.

SALMON GOUJONS WITH LIME AND CAPER DIP

THESE SCRUMPTIOUS SALMON STRIPS ARE COATED IN A MIXTURE OF POLENTA AND PAPRIKA BEFORE BEING FRIED. THIS GIVES THEM A REALLY CRISP FINISH WITH A SUBTLE SPICY FLAVOUR.

SERVES 4

INGREDIENTS
  350g/12oz salmon fillet, skinned
  50g/2oz/½ cup plain
    (all-purpose) flour
  2 eggs, beaten
  50g/2oz/⅓ cup polenta
  5ml/1 tsp paprika
  vegetable oil, for deep-frying
  salt and ground black pepper
  lime wedges, to garnish

For the dip
  200ml/7fl oz/scant 1 cup Greek
    (US strained plain) yogurt
  finely grated rind and juice of 1 lime
  30ml/2 tbsp drained capers,
    finely chopped

1 To make the dip, combine all the ingredients in a bowl and mix. Season and spoon into a serving dish. Cover and chill in the refrigerator.

2 Cut the salmon fillets into strips of 7.5 x 2.5cm/3 x 1in. Season the flour and place in a shallow dish. Pour the beaten egg into a separate shallow dish. Combine the polenta and paprika in a third shallow dish.

3 Dip the salmon strips, one at a time, in the seasoned flour, then in the beaten egg and finally in the polenta, making sure they are evenly coated.

4 Heat the oil for deep-frying until it is very hot. Fry the goujons in batches, about four or five at a time, for 3–5 minutes, turning them occasionally with a slotted spoon.

5 Remove the cooked goujons with a slotted spoon and drain well on a double thickness of kitchen paper. Keep the cooked goujons hot in the oven while you cook the remainder.

6 When all the goujons have been cooked, arrange them on a platter. Garnish them with the lime wedges and serve them with the lime and caper dip.

LOX WITH BAGELS AND CREAM CHEESE

THIS GLORIOUSLY COMFORTING, SELF-INDULGENT DISH IS PERFECT FOR A WEEKEND BREAKFAST OR A LIGHT LUNCH WITH FRIENDS. LOX IS THE JEWISH WORD FOR SMOKED SALMON, AND THIS RECIPE IS A REAL JEWISH DELI CLASSIC WHICH YOU CAN EASILY RECREATE AT HOME.

SERVES 2

INGREDIENTS

2 bagels
115–175g/4–6oz/½–¾ cup full-fat
  cream cheese
150g/5oz sliced best smoked salmon
ground black pepper
lemon wedges, to serve

1 Preheat the oven to 200ºC/400ºF/ Gas 6. Put the bagels on a large baking sheet and warm them in the oven for 4–5 minutes.

2 Remove the bagels from the oven, split them in two and spread generously with cream cheese. Pile the salmon on top of the bagels and grind over plenty of black pepper.

3 Squeeze over some lemon juice, then top with the other bagel half and eat while still warm.

4 For an easy and elegant touch, place a wedge of lemon in the centre of a small square of muslin (cheesecloth), bring up the edges to enclose it, tie with fine string and put it on the plate.

COOK'S TIP
It is essential to be generous with the smoked salmon and to use the best cream cheese you can find – absolutely not a low-fat version.

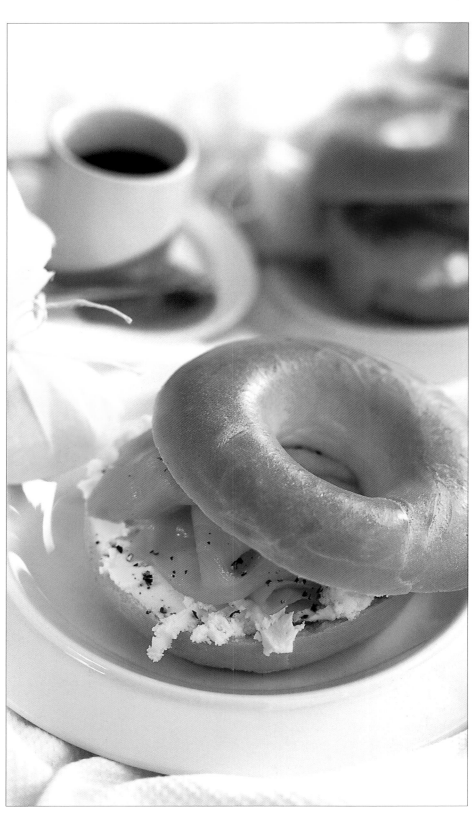

SMOKED FISH PLATTER <u>WITH</u> HONEY DRESSING

A WIDE VARIETY OF SMOKED FISH IS AVAILABLE TODAY — TROUT, SALMON AND MACKEREL FEATURE IN THIS SIMPLE APPETIZER — BUT ANY SMOKED FISH CAN BE USED. ASK YOUR LOCAL FISHMONGER OR INQUIRE AT THE FISH COUNTER AT THE SUPERMARKET FOR THE BEST BUYS.

SERVES 4

INGREDIENTS
½ Charentais melon
½ cantaloupe melon
50g/2oz rocket (arugula)
75g/3oz hot-smoked trout fillets
75g/3oz smoked salmon
75g/3oz smoked mackerel
  with peppercorns

For the dressing
75ml/5 tbsp extra virgin olive oil
15ml/1 tbsp white wine vinegar
5ml/1 tsp wholegrain mustard
5ml/1 tsp clear honey
salt and ground black pepper

COOK'S TIP
Among the more unusual types of smoked fish available are smoked halibut and smoked sturgeon. Smoked halibut has translucent white flesh and this, coupled with its delicate flavour, would make it a good addition to the fish platter. Smoked sturgeon would be a real talking point at any dinner table. A luxury fish, comparable with the finest smoked salmon, it is best served solo, so its rich flavour and succulent texture can be fully appreciated.

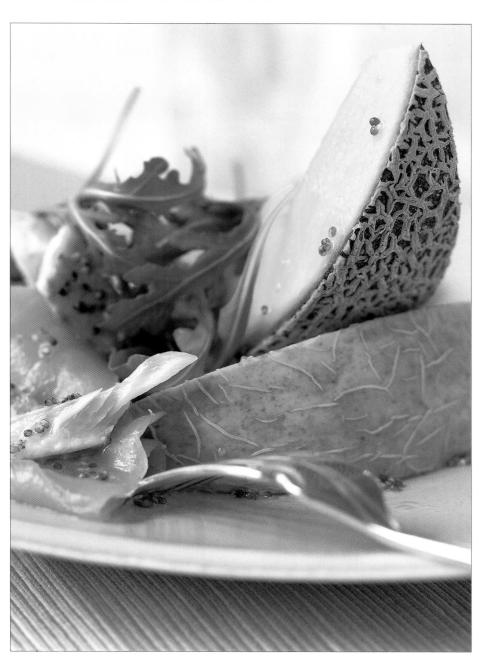

1 Scoop out and discard all the seeds from the Charentais and cantaloupe melons and cut each melon into four or eight slices, leaving the skin on. Divide the melon slices among four small serving plates, placing the slices neatly to one side.

2 Add a quarter of the rocket leaves to each plate, placing them opposite the melon.

3 Make the honey dressing by combining all the ingredients in a small jug (pitcher). Add plenty of salt and black pepper and whisk with a fork until emulsified.

4 Divide the smoked fish into four portions, breaking or cutting the trout fillets and smoked salmon into bitesize pieces. Peel the skin from the mackerel, then break up the flesh. Arrange the trout fillets, smoked salmon and mackerel over the rocket and melon on each platter. Drizzle the dressing over and serve immediately.

SALMON AU GRATIN

*THIS IS A VERY RICH APPETIZER, PERFECT FOR SERVING BEFORE
A RELATIVELY PLAIN MAIN COURSE, SUCH AS A SALAD. THE SALMON
IS BAKED IN A LUXURIOUS CREAM AND GRUYÈRE SAUCE.*

SERVES 6

INGREDIENTS
   350g/12oz salmon fillet, skinned
     and cubed
   grated rind and juice of 2 limes
   60ml/4 tbsp olive oil
   2 small red onions, sliced
   2 garlic cloves, finely chopped
   bunch of fresh tarragon, chopped
   450ml/¾ pint/scant 2 cups double
     (heavy) cream
   115g/4oz Gruyère cheese, grated
   salt and ground black pepper
   country bread, to serve

1 Place the salmon cubes in a bowl
and sprinkle the lime rind and juice
over. Toss well and leave to stand for
10 minutes. Meanwhile, use 15ml/1 tbsp
of the oil to lightly grease six ramekins.

2 Preheat the grill (broiler) to high. Heat
the remaining oil in a frying pan over a
medium heat, add the onion slices and
fry for 3 minutes. Add the garlic to the
pan and cook for a further 3 minutes,
taking care not to let it burn. Divide the
onion mixture among the ramekins.

3 Using a slotted spoon, remove the
salmon cubes from the marinade and
place them in a clean bowl. Add the
chopped tarragon and cream. Season
with salt and pepper and mix gently.

4 Divide among the ramekins and top
with the grated cheese. Support the
ramekins on a baking sheet and grill
(broil) for 5–6 minutes or until the
salmon is cooked and the cheese is
golden brown and bubbling. Serve
immediately with bread.

VARIATIONS
• Look out for salmon lardons in
specialist delicatessens. These, like
bacon lardons, are quite chunky, and
work well for a recipe like this. They
are popular in France, partly because
they are full of flavour and partly for
convenience, since they are ready cut.
• Although Gruyère is the preferred
cheese for these ramekins, Emmenthal
or Jarlsberg could be used instead. Grate
the cheese finely – a microplane grater
is useful for this.

SALMON PUFFS

CANNED SALMON IS CONVENIENT AND EASY TO USE. THE FLAVOUR AND TEXTURE ARE PERFECTLY ACCEPTABLE IN DISHES SUCH AS THIS ONE, WHERE THE FISH IS FLAKED AND MIXED WITH OTHER INGREDIENTS, INCLUDING SUN-DRIED TOMATOES, MAYONNAISE, LEMON AND CHOPPED PARSLEY.

SERVES 6–8

INGREDIENTS
  65g/2½oz/9 tbsp plain
    (all-purpose) flour
  50g/2oz/¼ cup butter
  150ml/¼ pint/⅔ cup water
  2 eggs, beaten
For the filling
  200g/7oz can red salmon, drained,
    or 175g/6oz poached salmon
  60ml/4 tbsp mayonnaise
  50g/2oz/⅓ cup sun-dried tomatoes
    in oil, drained and finely chopped
  grated rind and juice of ½ lemon
  30ml/2 tbsp freshly chopped parsley
  salt and ground black pepper
  salad leaves and halved cherry
    tomatoes, to serve

1 Sift the flour on to a sheet of baking parchment. Put the butter and water in a medium pan and heat gently until the butter melts. Bring to the boil and remove from the heat.

2 Immediately tip in all the flour and beat with a wooden spoon until the mixture forms a smooth, glossy paste. Leave the paste in a warm room to cool slightly for 5 minutes.

3 Meanwhile, make the filling. Flake the salmon finely and put it in a bowl. Add the mayonnaise, sun-dried tomatoes, lemon rind and juice. Stir in the parsley, with salt and pepper to taste. Cover and chill until ready to serve.

4 Add the beaten egg gradually to the cooled paste, stirring well after each addition to prevent the mixture from curdling. It may not be necessary to add all the egg; stir in just enough to produce a smooth, shiny mixture that is thick enough to hold its shape. Set the choux pastry aside.

5 Preheat the oven to 190°C/375°F/ Gas 5. Grease a large baking sheet. Carefully spoon the choux pastry into a piping (pastry) bag fitted with a 1cm/½in plain round nozzle.

6 Pipe the pastry on to the baking sheet to make about 24 small rounds, spaced well apart. Bake for 20–25 minutes until the puffs are browned.

7 Remove the puffs from the oven and split them horizontally in half to release the steam. Leave the puffs to cool completely on a wire rack.

8 Just before serving, use a teaspoon to fill each puff with a little of the salmon mixture. Divide the salad leaves and halved tomatoes among individual serving plates and place three or four puffs on each.

COOK'S TIPS
• It is essential that the oven has reached the required temperature before the puffs are baked, as they rely on that first burst of heat for the maximum rise.
• When making choux puffs, whether for a savoury or a sweet dish, always slit them to release the steam. If any uncooked paste remains in the centre, simply remove it and return the puffs to the oven for 2–3 minutes to dry out.

MAIN DISHES

We should be eating oily fish like salmon and trout at least two or three times a week, but although many of us intend to do just that, we sometimes get stuck in a recipe rut. There's a limit to how many times a person can serve fisherman's pie or grilled salmon, so this chapter introduces some delicious new recipes to expand your repertoire. Dishes like Salmon and Avocado Pizza, Herby Salmon Parcels, Coconut Salmon, and Salmon with Stilton are easy to prepare and taste great. Also on the menu are old favourites like Salmon Fish Cakes — served here with a spicy mayonnaise.

SALMON AND AVOCADO PIZZA

A MIXTURE OF SMOKED AND FRESH SALMON MAKES A DELICIOUS PIZZA TOPPING WHEN MIXED WITH AVOCADO. CAPERS ADD A TOUCH OF PIQUANCY TO CUT THE RICHNESS OF THE MAJOR INGREDIENTS.

SERVES 3–4

INGREDIENTS
    150g/5oz salmon fillet
    120ml/4fl oz/½ cup dry white wine
    15ml/1 tbsp olive oil
    400g/14oz can chopped
      tomatoes, drained
    115g/4oz mozzarella cheese, grated
    1 small avocado, halved, stoned
      (pitted), peeled and cubed
    10ml/2 tsp lemon juice
    30ml/2 tbsp crème fraîche or
      sour cream
    75g/3oz smoked salmon, cut
      into strips
    15ml/1 tbsp drained bottled capers
    30ml/2 tbsp chopped fresh chives,
      to garnish
    ground black pepper

For the pizza base
    175g/6oz/1½ cups strong white
      (bread) flour
    1.5ml/¼ tsp salt
    5ml/1 tsp easy-blend (rapid-rise)
      dried yeast
    120–150ml/4–5fl oz/½–⅔ cup
      lukewarm water
    15ml/1 tbsp olive oil

1 Make the pizza base. Sift the flour and salt into a mixing bowl, stir in the yeast, then make a well in the centre.

2 Add the lukewarm water to the well, then add the oil. Mix with a spoon gradually incorporating the flour to make a soft dough.

3 Knead the dough until smooth and elastic, then place in a bowl, cover with clear film (plastic wrap) and leave in a warm place for about 1 hour or until the dough has doubled in bulk.

4 Knock back (punch down) the dough, knead it briefly, then roll it out to a 25–30cm/10–12in round and support on a baking sheet. Push up the edges to make a rim.

5 Preheat the oven to 220°C/425°F/ Gas 7. Place the salmon in a frying pan, pour over the wine and season. Bring slowly to the boil, remove from the heat, cover and cool. (The fish will cook in the cooling liquid.) Skin and flake the salmon, removing any bones.

6 Brush the pizza base with the oil and spread over the drained tomatoes. Sprinkle over 50g/2oz of the mozzarella. Bake for 10 minutes. Meanwhile, toss the avocado in the lemon juice.

7 Dot teaspoonfuls of the crème fraîche or sour cream over the pizza base. Arrange the fresh and smoked salmon, avocado, capers and remaining mozzarella on top. Season with black pepper. Bake for a further 10 minutes until crisp and golden. Sprinkle over the chives and serve immediately.

COOK'S TIPS
• Smoked salmon trimmings are cheaper than smoked salmon slices and could be used for the topping.
• For an unusual addition to this pizza, try Peppadews. These sweet cherry chillies come from South Africa. There are mild and hot varieties, and both are delicious with salmon. Drain them thoroughly before cutting them into strips and adding them to the topping with the avocado and capers.
• When adding the topping, leave the rim of the pizza clear.

SALMON FISH CAKES

*WHOLEGRAIN MUSTARD GIVES THESE EXCELLENT FISH CAKES A
SLIGHT TANG, BARELY DETECTABLE BUT QUITE DELICIOUS. THE
FLAVOUR IS ECHOED IN THE MAYONNAISE THAT ACCOMPANIES
THEM. PEPPERY ROCKET IS THE PERFECT ACCOMPANIMENT.*

SERVES 4

INGREDIENTS

450g/1lb cooked salmon fillet
450g/1lb freshly cooked
  potatoes, mashed
25g/1oz/2 tbsp butter, melted
10ml/2 tsp wholegrain mustard
15ml/1 tbsp each chopped fresh dill
  and chopped fresh parsley
grated rind and juice of ½ lemon
15g/½oz/1 tbsp plain
  (all-purpose) flour
1 egg, lightly beaten
150g/5oz/1¼ cups home-made
  dried breadcrumbs
60ml/4 tbsp sunflower oil
salt and ground black pepper
rocket (arugula) leaves and chives,
  to garnish
lemon wedges, to serve

For the spicy mayonnaise
350ml/12fl oz/1½ cups mayonnaise
10ml/2 tsp wholegrain mustard
2.5–5ml/½–1 tsp Worcestershire
  sauce
dash of Tabasco sauce

COOK'S TIP
To make the dried breadcrumbs, crumb
day-old white bread in a food processor,
or grate it into a bowl. Spread out the
crumbs on baking sheets and dry in a
very low oven. Process again if you like,
to produce fine crumbs.

1 Flake the cooked salmon, discarding
any skin and bones. Put it in a bowl with
the mashed potato, melted butter and
wholegrain mustard, and mix well. Stir
in the dill, parsley, lemon rind and juice.
Season to taste with salt and pepper.

2 Divide the mixture into eight portions
and shape each into a ball, then flatten
into a thick disc. Dip the fish cakes
first in flour, then in egg and finally in
breadcrumbs, making sure that they
are evenly coated.

3 Put the salmon fish cakes on a plate
and place in the refrigerator to firm
up a little. Meanwhile, make the spicy
mayonnaise by mixing all the
ingredients in a bowl.

4 Heat the oil in a frying pan until it is
very hot. Fry the fish cakes in batches
until golden brown and crisp all over.
As each batch is ready, drain on kitchen
paper and keep hot while you fry the
rest. Garnish with rocket leaves and
chives and serve with the lemon wedges
and spicy mayonnaise.

SALMON BAKED WITH POTATOES AND THYME

THIS IS VERY SIMPLE AND ABSOLUTELY DELICIOUS. PEPPER-CRUSTED SALMON FILLETS ARE BAKED ON A BED OF POTATOES AND ONIONS BRAISED IN THYME-FLAVOURED VEGETABLE OR FISH STOCK.

SERVES 4

INGREDIENTS
  675g/1½lb waxy potatoes,
    thinly sliced
  1 onion, thinly sliced
  10ml/2 tsp fresh thyme leaves
  450ml/¾ pint/scant 2 cups vegetable
    or fish stock
  40g/1½oz/3 tbsp butter, finely diced
  4 salmon fillets, each about
    150g/5oz, skinned
  30ml/2 tbsp olive oil
  15ml/1 tbsp black peppercorns,
    roughly crushed
  salt and ground black pepper
  fresh thyme, to garnish
  mangetouts (snow peas) or sugar
    snap peas, to serve

1 Preheat the oven to 190ºC/375ºF/ Gas 5. Layer the potato and onion slices in a shallow baking dish, such as a lasagne dish, seasoning each layer and sprinkling with thyme. Pour over the stock, dot with butter, cover with foil and place in the oven.

2 Bake the potatoes for 40 minutes then remove the foil and bake for a further 20 minutes, or until they are almost cooked.

3 Meanwhile brush the salmon fillets with olive oil and coat with crushed black peppercorns, pressing them in, if necessary, with the back of a spoon.

4 Place the salmon on top of the potatoes, cover with foil and bake for 15 minutes, or until the salmon is opaque, removing the foil for the last 5 minutes. Garnish with fresh thyme sprigs and serve with mangetouts or sugar snap peas.

SALMON AND BLACK-EYED BEAN STEW

THE ADDITION OF FRESH SALMON TO THIS STEW HELPS TO MAKE IT AN EXTREMELY NOURISHING DISH, AS WELL AS A DELICIOUS WINTER WARMER. THE CANNED BEANS ARE AN ADDED ENERGY BOOST.

SERVES 2

INGREDIENTS

150g/5oz salmon fillet, skinned and
   any bones removed
400g/14oz canned black-eyed beans
   (peas) in brine
50g/2oz fresh shiitake mushrooms,
   stalks removed
1 small carrot, peeled
½ mooli (daikon), peeled
5g/⅛oz dashi-konbu (dried kelp
   seaweed), about 10cm/4in square
60ml/4 tbsp water
15ml/1 tbsp shoyu (Japanese
   soy sauce)
7.5ml/1½ tsp mirin or dry sherry
sea salt
2.5cm/1in fresh root ginger, peeled,
   to garnish

1 Slice the salmon into 1cm/½in-thick strips. Place in a colander, sprinkle with sea salt and leave for 1 hour.

2 Wash away the salt and cut the salmon strips into 1cm/½in cubes. Par-boil in a pan of rapidly boiling water for 30 seconds, then drain. Gently rinse under cold running water to prevent the cubes from cooking further.

3 Slice the ginger for the garnish thinly lengthways, then stack the slices and cut them into thin threads. Soak in cold water for about 30 minutes, then drain well.

4 Drain the can of black-eyed beans into a medium pan. Reserve the beans.

5 Chop all the fresh vegetables into 1cm/½in cubes. Wipe the dashi-konbu with kitchen paper, then snip with scissors. Cut everything as close to the same size as possible.

6 Put the par-boiled salmon, dashi-konbu and vegetables into the pan containing the liquid from the can of beans. Pour the beans on top and add the 60ml/4 tbsp water and 1.5ml/¼ tsp salt. Bring to the boil. Reduce the heat to low and cook for 6 minutes or until the carrot is cooked.

7 Add the shoyu and cook for a further 4 minutes. Add the mirin or sherry and remove the pan from the heat. Mix well. Leave to rest for 1 hour. Serve warm or cold, with the ginger threads.

HERBY SALMON PARCELS

COOKING SALMON, OR ANY FISH, IN A PARCEL HELPS TO KEEP IT MOIST AND SEALS IN ALL THE WONDERFUL FLAVOURS. ADDING LIME AND BASIL TO THE PAPER-WRAPPED SALMON GIVES THE FISH A FRESH, TANGY TASTE.

SERVES 4

INGREDIENTS
    1 lime
    50g/2oz/¼ cup butter, softened
    30ml/2 tbsp finely chopped
      fresh basil
    4 plum tomatoes, sliced
    2 garlic cloves, sliced
    4 salmon fillets, each about
      200g/7oz
    15ml/1 tbsp olive oil

1 Grate the rind from the lime and put it in a small bowl. Cut the lime into eight slices and set aside. Add the butter and basil to the lime rind and mix well. Roll the mixture into a cylinder shape, wrap in greaseproof (waxed) paper or baking parchment and chill in the refrigerator.

2 Preheat the oven to 190°C/375°F/ Gas 5. Cut out sheets of greaseproof paper or baking parchment, each large enough to enclose a salmon fillet easily.

COOK'S TIP
The flavour of the tomatoes is central to the success of this dish. If you can obtain home-grown Italian plum tomatoes, such as San Morzano, so much the better. Alternatively, plump for sweet and juicy cherry tomatoes.

3 Arrange one sliced tomato on each piece of paper or parchment. Sprinkle each with one-quarter of the garlic and season with plenty of salt and pepper.

4 Place the salmon fillets on the tomatoes. Cut the chilled, flavoured butter into four equal pieces and place one on each salmon. Top with the reserved lime slices and drizzle the salmon evenly with the olive oil.

5 Fold the paper or parchment around the topped salmon to make neat parcels. Place on a baking sheet and bake for 20 minutes or until the fish is cooked through.

SALMON WITH LEEKS AND PEPPERS

COOKING SALMON IN PAPER PARCELS IS A HEALTHY OPTION. THE FISH AND VEGETABLES COOK IN THEIR OWN JUICES, SO BOTH RETAIN ALL THEIR VALUABLE NUTRIENTS.

SERVES 6

INGREDIENTS

    25ml/1½ tbsp groundnut (peanut) oil
    2 yellow (bell) peppers, seeded and
       thinly sliced
    4cm/1½in fresh root ginger, peeled
       and finely shredded
    1 large fennel bulb, thinly sliced,
       fronds chopped and reserved
    1 fresh green chilli, seeded and
       finely shredded
    2 large leeks, cut into 10cm/4in
       lengths and shredded lengthways
    30ml/2 tbsp chopped fresh chives
    10ml/2 tsp light soy sauce
    6 portions salmon fillet, each
       weighing about 150–175g/
       5–6oz, skinned
    10ml/2 tsp toasted sesame oil
    salt and ground black pepper

1 Heat the oil in a large frying pan. Add the yellow peppers, ginger and fennel bulb and cook, stirring occasionally, for 5–6 minutes, until they are softened, but not browned.

2 Add the chilli and leeks to the pan and cook, stirring occasionally, for about 3 minutes. Stir in half the chopped chives and the soy sauce and season to taste with a little salt and pepper. Set the vegetable mixture aside to cool slightly.

3 Preheat the oven to 190°C/375°F/ Gas 5. Cut six 35cm/14in rounds of baking parchment or foil and set aside.

4 When the vegetable mixture is cool, divide it equally among the paper or foil rounds and top each with a piece of salmon fillet.

5 Drizzle each portion of fish with a little sesame oil and sprinkle with the remaining chives and the chopped fennel fronds. Season with a little more salt and ground black pepper.

6 Fold the baking parchment or foil over to enclose the fish, rolling and twisting the edges together to seal the parcels.

7 Place the parcels on a baking sheet and bake for 15–20 minutes, or until the parcels have puffed up. Carefully transfer the parcels to six warmed plates and serve immediately, to be opened at the table.

PAN-FRIED SALMON WITH MUSHROOM SAUCE

TARRAGON HAS A DISTINCTIVE ANISEED FLAVOUR THAT IS GREAT WITH SALMON. HERE IT IS USED, NOT WITH THE FISH, BUT IN THE EXQUISITE WILD AND FRESH MUSHROOM SAUCE THAT ACCOMPANIES IT.

SERVES 4

INGREDIENTS

50g/2oz/¼ cup butter
salt and cayenne pepper
4 salmon steaks, each 175g/6oz
1 shallot, finely chopped
175g/6oz/about 2½ cups assorted
  wild and cultivated mushrooms,
  trimmed and sliced
200ml/7fl oz/scant 1 cup chicken
  or vegetable stock
10ml/2 tsp cornflour (cornstarch)
2.5ml/½ tsp mustard powder
15ml/1 tbsp water
50ml/3½ tbsp sour cream
45ml/3 tbsp chopped fresh tarragon
5ml/1 tsp white wine vinegar

1 Melt half the butter in a large frying pan. Season the salmon, add the steaks to the pan and cook, in batches if necessary, over a medium heat for 8 minutes, turning once. Transfer to a plate, cover and keep warm.

2 Heat the remaining butter in the pan and gently fry the shallot until softened but not coloured. Add the mushrooms and cook until the juices begin to flow.

3 Add the stock and simmer for 2–3 minutes. Put the cornflour and mustard powder in a cup and mix to a paste with the water. Stir into the mushroom mixture and bring to a simmer, stirring until the sauce thickens. Stir in the sour cream, tarragon and vinegar. Season the sauce with salt and cayenne pepper.

4 Spoon the mushroom sauce over each salmon steak and serve with new potatoes and a green salad.

COOK'S TIP
Fresh tarragon will bruise and darken quickly after chopping, so prepare the herb only when you are ready to use it.

SALMON WITH WHISKY AND CREAM

THIS DISH COMBINES TWO OF THE FINEST FLAVOURS OF SCOTLAND — SALMON AND WHISKY. IT TAKES VERY LITTLE TIME TO MAKE, SO COOK IT AT THE LAST MOMENT. SERVE QUITE PLAINLY.

SERVES 4

INGREDIENTS

   4 thin pieces of salmon fillet, about
     175g/6oz each
   5ml/1 tsp chopped fresh
     thyme leaves
   50g/2oz/¼ cup butter
   75ml/5 tbsp whisky
   150ml/¼ pint/⅔ cup double
     (heavy) cream
   juice of ½ lemon (optional)
   salt and ground black pepper
   fresh dill sprigs, to garnish

1 Season the salmon with salt, pepper and thyme. Melt half the butter in a frying pan large enough to hold two pieces of salmon side by side.

2 When the butter is foaming, fry the first two pieces of salmon for 2–3 minutes on each side, until they are golden on the outside and just cooked through.

3 Pour in 30ml/2 tbsp of the whisky and ignite it. When the flames have died down, carefully transfer the salmon to a plate and keep it hot. Heat the remaining butter and cook the second two pieces of salmon in the same way. Keep them hot.

4 Pour the cream into the pan and bring to the boil, stirring constantly and scraping up the cooking juices from the base of the pan. Allow to bubble until reduced and slightly thickened, then season and add the last of the whisky and a squeeze of lemon if you like.

5 Place the salmon pieces on individual warmed plates, pour the sauce over and garnish with dill. New potatoes and crisp green beans are good with this.

SALMON <u>WITH</u> GREEN PEPPERCORNS

SALMON BENEFITS FROM BEING SERVED WITH A PIQUANT ACCOMPANIMENT. LEMON AND LIME ARE THE OBVIOUS CHOICES, BUT CAPERS AND GREEN PEPPERCORNS ALSO SERVE TO COUNTER THE RICH TASTE.

<u>SERVES 4</u>

INGREDIENTS
15g/½oz/1 tbsp butter
2–3 shallots, finely chopped
15ml/1 tbsp brandy (optional)
60ml/4 tbsp white wine
90ml/6 tbsp fish or chicken stock
120ml/4fl oz/½ cup whipping cream
30–45ml/2–3 tbsp green peppercorns
     in brine, rinsed
15–30ml/1–2 tbsp vegetable oil
4 pieces salmon fillet, each about
     175g/6oz
salt and ground black pepper
fresh parsley, to garnish

1 Melt the butter in a heavy pan over a medium heat. Add the shallots and cook for 1–2 minutes, until just softened but not coloured.

2 Add the brandy, if using, then pour in the white wine and stock. Bring to the boil. Boil vigorously to reduce by three-quarters, stirring occasionally.

3 Reduce the heat, then add the cream and half the peppercorns, crushing them slightly against the sides of the pan with the back of a spoon. Cook very gently for 4–5 minutes, until the sauce has thickened slightly,

4 Strain the sauce into a clean pan and stir in the remaining peppercorns. Keep the sauce warm over a very low heat, stirring occasionally, while you cook the salmon fillets.

5 Heat the oil in a large, heavy frying pan over a medium-high heat. Lightly season the salmon. When the oil is very hot, add the salmon. Sear the fillets on both sides, then lower the heat and cook for 4–6 minutes, until the flesh is opaque throughout. Arrange the fish on warmed plates and pour over the sauce. Garnish with parsley and serve.

COOK'S TIP
Green peppercorns are available pickled in jars or cans. Keep them on hand for adding to all kinds of sauces and stews. Rinse the peppercorns before use.

MONGOLIAN FIREPOT

A FIREPOT PROVIDES A WONDERFUL WAY TO ENTERTAIN. AS WITH FONDUE RECIPES, THE FOOD IS COOKED AT THE TABLE, BUT IN THE HEALTHIER MEDIUM OF STOCK RATHER THAN OIL. AS A BONUS, THIS BECOMES A FLAVOURSOME BROTH WHICH IS DRUNK AT THE CONCLUSION OF THE MEAL.

SERVES 4–6

INGREDIENTS

2 salmon or tuna fillets, each about 150g/5oz, skinned
8–12 whole raw tiger or king prawns (jumbo shrimp), peeled and deveined, with tails on
6 sachets instant miso soup mixed with 1.75 litres/3 pints/7½ cups water or the same quantity of fish, chicken or vegetable stock
handful of coriander (cilantro) leaves
2–3 spring onions (scallions), sliced
small bunch watercress, rocket (arugula) or young mizuna greens
50g/2oz/¾ cup enoki mushrooms
200g/7oz fine egg noodles
8–12 lemon grass stalks or wooden skewers
soy sauce and wasabi paste or horseradish sauce, to serve

For the marinade
grated rind and juice of 2 limes
30ml/2 tbsp soy sauce
2.5cm/1in piece fresh root ginger, peeled and finely chopped
2 garlic cloves, finely chopped
15ml/1 tbsp clear honey
1 fresh red chilli, seeded and chopped

1 Cut the salmon or tuna fillets into 2.5cm/1in cubes and place in a deep serving bowl. Wash the prawns, pat them dry using kitchen paper, then add them to the fish cubes.

2 Mix all the marinade ingredients together and add to the bowl of seafood. Toss gently to coat, then cover and leave the seafood to marinate in the refrigerator for a minimum of 10 minutes, or 2 hours if possible.

3 Pour the stock into a pan, add the coriander and spring onions and bring to the boil. Transfer to a fondue pot and place on a burner at the table or pour the stock into a firepot at the table and keep hot.

4 Arrange the salad leaves and mushrooms on serving plates, and put the soy sauce and wasabi or horseradish into small bowls. Add the noodles to the stock at the table and leave to cook.

5 Invite each diner to spear a cube of fish or a prawn on a lemon grass stalk or skewer with a salad leaf and a mushroom. This is then submerged in the stock for 1 minute, or until the fish or prawn is cooked, then dipped into the soy sauce and wasabi or horseradish.

6 When the fish and vegetables have all been eaten, serve the remaining stock and noodles in soup bowls.

COOK'S TIP
To make them easier to eat, snip the noodles into short lengths using a pair of scissors.

COCONUT SALMON

SALMON IS QUITE A ROBUST FISH, AND RESPONDS WELL TO BEING COOKED WITH STRONG FLAVOURS,
AS IN THIS FRAGRANT BLEND OF SPICES, GARLIC AND CHILLI. COCONUT MILK ADDS A MELLOW TOUCH.

SERVES 4

INGREDIENTS
   4 salmon steaks, each about
     175g/6oz
   10ml/2 tsp ground cumin
   10ml/2 tsp chilli powder
   2.5ml/½ tsp ground turmeric
   30ml/2 tbsp white wine vinegar
   1.5ml/¼ tsp salt
   45ml/3 tbsp oil
   1 onion, chopped
   2 fresh green chillies, seeded
     and chopped
   2 garlic cloves, crushed
   2.5cm/1in piece fresh root
     ginger, grated
   5ml/1 tsp ground coriander
   175ml/6fl oz/¾ cup coconut milk
   fresh coriander (cilantro) sprigs,
     to garnish
   rice with spring onions (scallions),
     to serve

1 Arrange the salmon steaks in a single layer in a shallow glass dish. Put 5ml/ 1 tsp of the ground cumin in a bowl and add the chilli powder, turmeric, vinegar and salt. Rub the paste over the salmon steaks and leave to marinate for about 15 minutes.

2 Heat the oil in a large deep frying pan and fry the onion, chillies, garlic and ginger for 5–6 minutes. Put into a food processor or blender and process to a smooth paste.

3 Return the onion paste to the pan. Add the remaining cumin, the coriander and coconut milk. Bring to the boil, reduce the heat and simmer the sauce for 5 minutes, stirring occasionally.

4 Add the salmon steaks. Cover and cook for 15 minutes, until the fish is tender. Transfer to a serving dish and garnish with the fresh coriander. Serve with the rice and spring onions.

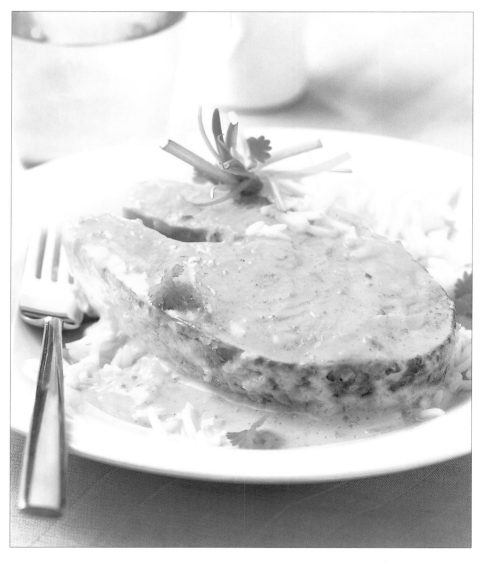

ASIAN SEARED SALMON

SALMON FILLETS ONLY TAKE A FEW MINUTES TO COOK, BUT MAKE SURE YOU ALLOW ENOUGH TIME FOR THE FISH TO SOAK UP ALL THE FLAVOURS OF THE MARINADE BEFORE YOU START COOKING.

SERVES 4

INGREDIENTS
    grated rind and juice of 1 lime
    15ml/1 tbsp soy sauce
    2 spring onions (scallions), sliced
    1 fresh red chilli, seeded and
      finely chopped
    2.5cm/1in piece fresh root ginger,
      peeled and grated
    1 lemon grass stalk, finely chopped
    4 salmon fillets, each about
      175g/6oz
    30ml/2 tbsp olive oil
    salt and ground black pepper
    45ml/3 tbsp fresh coriander
      (cilantro), to garnish

For the noodles
    250g/9oz medium egg noodles
    30ml/2 tbsp olive oil
    1 carrot, cut into fine strips
    1 red (bell) pepper, seeded and cut
      into fine strips
    1 yellow (bell) pepper, seeded and
      cut into fine strips
    115g/4oz mangetouts (snow peas)
    15ml/1 tbsp sesame oil

1 Put the grated lime rind in a jug (pitcher) and pour in the lime juice. Add the soy sauce, spring onions, chilli, ginger and lemon grass. Season with pepper and stir well. Place the salmon in a shallow non-metallic dish and pour the lime mixture over. Cover and marinate in the refrigerator for at least 30 minutes.

2 Bring a large pan of lightly salted water to the boil and cook the noodles according to the instructions on the packet. Drain well and set aside.

COOK'S TIP
Fresh root ginger is a wonderful ingredient. Thin slices can be added to boiling water to make a refreshing tea, and grated ginger makes a great addition to curries and stir-fries. Ginger freezes successfully and can be shaved or grated from frozen.

3 Brush a griddle pan with 15ml/1 tbsp of the olive oil and heat until hot. Remove the fish from the marinade, pat dry and add to the griddle pan. Cook the salmon fillets for 6 minutes, turning once.

4 When the salmon is almost cooked, add to the remaining marinade in a separate pan and heat through.

5 While the fish is cooking, heat the remaining oil in a wok or large frying pan. Add the carrot and stir-fry for 3 minutes. Add the drained noodles, pepper strips and mangetouts and toss over the heat for 2 minutes more. Drizzle the sesame oil over and season well.

6 Serve the salmon on a bed of noodles and vegetables. Garnish with coriander.

SALMON AND SCALLOP BROCHETTES

USING LEMON GRASS AS SKEWERS ISN'T A CULINARY GIMMICK. THE SUBTLE FLAVOUR GIVES THE INGREDIENTS — IN THIS CASE, SALMON AND SCALLOPS — A FRAGRANCE THAT SEEMS PERFECTLY IN KEEPING WITH THE DELICACY OF THIS SUPERB DINNER DISH.

SERVES 4

INGREDIENTS
8 lemon grass stalks
225g/8oz salmon fillet, skinned
8 queen scallops, with their corals
  if possible
8 baby onions, peeled and blanched
½ yellow (bell) pepper, cut into
  eight squares
100g/4oz/½ cup butter
juice of ½ lemon
30ml/2 tbsp dry vermouth
5ml/1 tsp chopped fresh tarragon
salt, ground white pepper
  and paprika

1 Preheat the grill (broiler) to medium-high. Cut off the top 7.5–10cm/3–4in of each lemon grass stalk. Reserve the bulb ends for another dish. Cut the salmon fillet into twelve 2cm/¾in cubes. Thread the salmon, scallops, corals if available, onions and pepper squares on to the lemon grass sticks and arrange the brochettes side by side in a grill (broiler) pan.

2 Melt half the butter in a small pan, add the lemon juice and a pinch of paprika and then brush all over the brochettes. Grill (broil) the skewers for about 2–3 minutes on each side, turning and basting the brochettes every minute, until the fish and scallops are just cooked, but are still very juicy. Transfer to a platter and keep hot while you make the tarragon butter sauce.

3 Pour the dry vermouth and all the leftover cooking juices from the brochettes into a small pan and boil quite fiercely to reduce by half. Add the remaining butter and melt, stirring all the time. Stir in the chopped fresh tarragon and add salt and ground white pepper to taste. Pour the tarragon butter sauce over the brochettes and serve immediately.

CLASSIC FISH PIE

ORIGINALLY A FISH PIE WAS BASED ON THE "CATCH OF THE DAY". SALMON WAS SELDOM INCLUDED, AS IT WAS TOO EXPENSIVE. NOW THAT GOOD QUALITY FARMED SALMON IS AVAILABLE — AND AFFORDABLE — IT MAKES AN EXCELLENT ADDITION TO THE OTHER FISH USED.

SERVES 4

INGREDIENTS
    butter, for greasing
    450g/1lb mixed fish, including
        salmon fillets
    finely grated rind of 1 lemon
    450g/1lb floury potatoes, peeled
    25g/1oz/2 tbsp butter
    salt and ground black pepper
    1 egg, beaten

For the sauce
    15g/½oz/1 tbsp butter
    15ml/1 tbsp plain (all-purpose) flour
    150ml/¼ pint/⅔ cup milk
    45ml/3 tbsp chopped fresh parsley

1 Preheat the oven to 220°C/425°F/ Gas 7. Grease a baking dish and set aside. Cut the fish into bitesize pieces. Season the fish, sprinkle over the lemon rind and place in the base of the prepared dish.

2 Put the potatoes in a pan. Add cold water to cover and bring to the boil. Cook for 25–30 minutes until tender.

3 Meanwhile, make the sauce. Melt the butter in a pan, add the flour and cook, stirring, for 2–3 minutes. Gradually add the milk, whisking constantly until the mixture boils and thickens to make a smooth white sauce.

4 Stir in the parsley and season to taste. Pour over the fish and mix gently.

5 Drain the potatoes well, return to the pan and mash with the butter.

6 Pipe or spoon the mashed potato on top of the fish mixture. Brush with the beaten egg. Bake for 45 minutes until the potato topping is golden brown. Serve hot.

COOK'S TIP
If using frozen fish thaw it very well and drain it thoroughly, as excess water will ruin the pie.

SALMON QUICHE <u>WITH</u> POTATO PASTRY

THERE ARE SO MANY WONDERFUL WAYS OF USING SMOKED SALMON. HERE IT FORMS THE FILLING FOR
A LIGHT BUT RICHLY-FLAVOURED QUICHE MADE WITH MELT-IN-THE-MOUTH POTATO PASTRY.

SERVES 6

INGREDIENTS
    115g/4oz floury potatoes, diced
    225g/8oz/2 cups plain (all-purpose)
      flour, sifted
    115g/4oz/½ cup butter, diced
    ½ egg, beaten
    10ml/2 tsp chilled water
    salad leaves and chopped fresh dill,
      to serve

For the filling
    6 eggs, beaten
    150ml/¼ pint/⅔ cup full cream
      (whole) milk
    300ml/½ pint/1¼ cups double
      (heavy) cream
    30–45ml/2–3 tbsp chopped fresh dill
    30ml/2 tbsp drained bottled
      capers, chopped
    275g/10oz smoked salmon
    salt and ground black pepper

1 Cook the potatoes in a large pan of lightly salted boiling water for 15 minutes or until tender. Drain well through a colander and return to the pan. Mash the potatoes until smooth and set aside to cool completely.

2 Place the flour in a bowl and rub or cut in the butter to form fine crumbs. Beat in the potatoes and egg. Bring the mixture together, adding chilled water if needed.

3 Roll the pastry out on a floured surface to a 28cm/11in round. Lop the pastry over the rolling pin and ease it into a deep, 23cm/9in round, loose-based, fluted quiche pan. Trim the edges. Chill for 1 hour.

4 Preheat the oven to 200°C/400°F/ Gas 6. Place a baking sheet in the oven to heat it. Using a sharp cook's knife or a pair of kitchen scissors, chop the salmon into bitesize pieces. Place the salmon on a plate and set it aside.

5 Make the filling. In a bowl, beat the eggs with the milk and cream. Stir in the dill and capers and season with pepper. Add in the salmon and stir to combine.

6 Remove the pastry case (pie shell) from the refrigerator, prick the base well and pour the mixture into it. Bake on a baking sheet for 35–45 minutes. Serve warm with mixed salad leaves and some more dill.

VARIATIONS
These quantities can also be used to make six individual quiches, which are an ideal size to serve as a first course or a light lunch. Prepare them as above, but reduce the cooking time by about 15 minutes. For extra piquancy, sprinkle some finely grated fresh Parmesan cheese over the top of each quiche before baking in the oven.

COOK'S TIP
To ensure the pastry base or the quiche cooks through it is vital to preheat the baking sheet in the oven first.

SALMON PASTRY <u>WITH</u> CHANTERELLE CREAM

*SPECTACULAR IS AN APT ADJECTIVE TO DESCRIBE THIS DISH, WHICH NOT ONLY LOOKS MAGNIFICENT
BUT ALSO TASTES SUPERB, WITH THE CRISP PUFF PASTRY PROVIDING A CONTRAST TO THE CREAMY
MUSHROOM FILLING AND FLAVOURSOME FISH.*

<u>SERVES 6</u>

INGREDIENTS

2 packets puff pastry, each
350g/12oz, thawed if frozen
1 egg, beaten, to glaze
2 large salmon fillets, total weight
about 900g/2lb, skinned
375ml/13fl oz/generous 1½ cups dry
white wine
1 small carrot
1 small onion, halved
½ celery stick, chopped
1 fresh thyme sprig

For the chanterelle cream

25g/1oz/2 tbsp unsalted
(sweet) butter
2 shallots, chopped
225g/8oz/3 cups chanterelles or
mixed wild mushrooms, trimmed
and sliced
75ml/5 tbsp white wine
150ml/¼ pint/⅔ cup double
(heavy) cream
45ml/3 tbsp chopped fresh chervil
30ml/2 tbsp chopped fresh chives

For the hollandaise sauce

2 egg yolks
10ml/2 tsp lemon juice, plus more
to taste, if needed
115g/4oz/½ cup unsalted (sweet)
butter, melted
salt and ground black pepper

COOK'S TIP

If the salmon fillet breaks in half as you
lift it out of the roasting pan, don't worry.
Just reassemble the fish on the pastry.
The mushroom cream will mask any
obvious joins.

VARIATION

Instead of adding the butter to the
egg mixture in the bowl, you could
put the mixture in a food processor
and add the butter through the feeder
tube with the motor running.

1 Roll out the pastry on a floured
surface to a rectangle 10cm/4in longer
and 5cm/2in wider than the salmon
fillets. Trim into a fish shape, support
on a large baking sheet, decorate with a
pastry cutter and glaze with beaten egg.
Chill for 1 hour.

2 Preheat the oven to 200°C/400°F/
Gas 6. Bake the pastry for 30–35
minutes until well risen and golden.
Remove from the oven and carefully
split in half horizontally to provide two
matching fish shapes. Reduce the oven
temperature to 160°C/325°F/Gas 3.

3 Make the chanterelle cream. Melt
the butter in a heavy pan and fry the
shallots gently until soft but not
coloured. Add the mushrooms and
cook until their juices begin to run.

4 Pour in the wine, increase the heat
and cook until the juices have
evaporated. When the mushroom
mixture is quite dry, stir in the cream
and herbs and bring to a simmer.
Season well, transfer to a bowl, cover
and keep warm.

5 To poach the salmon fillets, place
them in a roasting pan. Add the wine,
carrot, onion, celery, thyme and enough
water to cover the fish completely.

6 Bring to the boil slowly. As soon as
the water begins to tremble, remove
from the heat, cover with a tight-fitting
lid or foil and set the pan aside for
30 minutes. The fish will continue to
cook in the residual heat.

7 Carefully lift out the salmon fillets,
draining them well. Put the base of
the pastry on a baking sheet and lay
a salmon fillet on top. Spread with the
chanterelle cream and cover with a
second salmon fillet. Cover with the top
of the pastry "fish" and warm through
in the oven for 10–15 minutes.

8 For the hollandaise sauce, pour the
melted butter in a steady stream on to
the egg yolk mixture in a heatproof bowl
set over a pan of boiling water. Beat
vigorously with a whisk to make a
smooth, creamy sauce. Taste the sauce
and add salt, pepper and more lemon
juice if needed. Serve with the pastry.

SALMON COULIBIAC

THIS IS A COMPLICATED RUSSIAN DISH THAT TAKES A LOT OF PREPARATION, BUT IT IS WELL WORTH IT. TRADITIONALLY, STURGEON IS USED, BUT SALMON MAKES AN EXCELLENT ALTERNATIVE.

SERVES 8

INGREDIENTS
   butter, for greasing
   flour, for dusting
   450g/1lb puff pastry
   1 egg, beaten
   salt and ground black pepper
   lemon wedges and fresh dill sprigs,
    to garnish

For the filling
   50g/2oz/¼ cup butter
   350g/12oz/5 cups chestnut
    mushrooms, sliced
   105ml/7 tbsp white wine
   juice of ½ lemon
   675g/1½lb salmon fillet, skinned
   115g/4oz/scant ½ cup long grain rice
   30ml/2 tbsp chopped fresh dill
   1 large onion, chopped
   4 hard-boiled eggs, shelled
    and sliced

1 First make the filling. Melt most of the butter in a frying pan that is large enough to accommodate the salmon. Add the mushrooms and cook for 3 minutes. Pour in 60ml/4 tbsp of the wine and boil for 2 minutes, then simmer for 5 minutes. Stir in almost all of the remaining wine and the lemon juice.

2 Place the salmon on top of the cooked mushrooms, cover with foil and steam gently for 8–10 minutes, until just cooked. Remove the salmon from the pan and set aside.

3 With a slotted spoon, transfer the mushrooms to a bowl. Pour the cooking liquid into a large pan. Add the rice and cook for 10–15 minutes, until tender, adding water or more wine if needed.

4 Remove from the heat and stir in the dill and seasoning. Melt the remaining butter and fry the onion until golden brown. Set aside.

5 Grease a large baking sheet. Using baking parchment, cut out a fish-shaped template that will fit easily on the baking sheet. Roll out just less than half the pastry and use the template to cut a fish shape. Place on the baking sheet.

6 Leaving the edges clear, spread out half the mushrooms on the pastry and top with half the rice, half the onion and half the eggs. Place the salmon on top, cutting it to fit if necessary, then repeat the layers in reverse.

7 Roll out the remaining pastry and cut a slightly larger fish shape than before, so that it will cover the filling. Brush the base pastry rim with beaten egg, fit the pastry top in place and seal the edges. Chill for 1 hour.

8 Preheat the oven to 220°C/425°F/ Gas 7. Cut four small slits in the top of the pastry, brush with more egg and bake for 10 minutes. Reduce the oven temperature to 190°C/375°F/Gas 5 and bake for 30 minutes more, until golden. Garnish with lemon and dill and serve.

PEPPERED SALMON STEAKS

PINK PEPPERCORNS NOT ONLY MATCH THE DELICATE COLOUR OF SALMON, BUT ALSO COMPLEMENT ITS FLAVOUR. THIS IS A LIGHT DISH, WHICH LOOKS VERY PRETTY WITH ITS SMOKED SALMON TOPPING.

2 Sprinkle the dill over the leeks and courgettes and put the salmon steaks in a single layer on top.

3 Place the pink peppercorns in a mortar and crush them lightly with a pestle until about half the corns are broken. Top the salmon with the peppercorns and the bay leaves.

4 Pour the wine over the steaks and dot with the butter. Season well, cover tightly using foil and bake for 20–25 minutes.

SERVES 4

INGREDIENTS

1 leek, cut into fine strips
2 courgettes (zucchini), cut into
  fine strips
15ml/1 tbsp olive oil
15ml/1 tbsp chopped fresh dill
4 salmon steaks
10ml/2 tsp pink peppercorns
8 small bay leaves
150ml/¼ pint/⅔ cup dry white wine
15g/½oz/1 tbsp butter
50g/2oz smoked salmon
20ml/4 tsp salmon roe
salt and ground black pepper

1 Preheat the oven to 190°C/375°F/ Gas 5. Mix the leek and courgette strips with the oil in a bowl. Toss to coat, then spread out on the base of a shallow baking dish.

5 Cut the smoked salmon into strips. Serve each steak on a bed of the braised leek and courgette mixture and top each portion with smoked salmon strips and salmon roe.

SALMON WITH STILTON

*A RICH BLUE STILTON AND HERB BUTTER MAKES A FLAVOURSOME
SAUCE FOR SALMON STEAKS BAKED IN WINE. SERVE THIS TOTALLY
MOUTHWATERING MELANGE WITH NEW POTATOES, STIR-FRIED RED
AND YELLOW PEPPERS AND MANGETOUTS.*

SERVES 4

INGREDIENTS
  115g/4oz Stilton cheese
  25g/1oz/2 tbsp butter, softened
  15ml/1 tbsp chopped fresh chives,
    plus extra, to garnish
  15ml/1 tbsp chopped fresh
    thyme leaves
  1 garlic clove, crushed
  30ml/2 tbsp olive oil
  4 salmon steaks
  60ml/4 tbsp dry white wine
  salt and ground black pepper
  new potatoes and stir-fried red and
    yellow (bell) peppers and
    mangetouts (snow peas), to serve

1 Crumble the Stilton and place it in a
food processor with the softened butter.
Process until smooth. Scrape the Stilton
butter into a small bowl.

2 Stir in the 15ml/1 tbsp chives, with
the thyme and garlic. Season to taste.
Stilton is salty, so you will probably only
need to add pepper. Preheat the oven
to 180°C/350°F/Gas 4.

3 Place the butter on a piece of foil
and shape into an oblong. Wrap this in
the foil and seal tightly. Chill the butter
by placing it in the refrigerator until it
is firm.

4 Brush a sheet of foil, large enough
to enclose all the steaks, with olive oil.
Support the foil on a baking sheet.
Place the steaks on the foil, drizzle the
wine over, season and seal the foil
tightly. Bake for 20–30 minutes or until
cooked through.

5 Unwrap the chilled butter and cut
it into four equal portions. Remove the
salmon from the oven, carefully open
the package and use a fish slice (metal
spatula) to transfer each steak to a
warmed serving plate.

6 Top each salmon steak with a portion
of butter and garnish with the extra
chives. Serve immediately with new
potatoes and stir-fried red and yellow
peppers and mangetouts.

COOK'S TIPS
• If your food processor has a mini bowl
for small quantities, use that when
making the Stilton butter.
• When wrapping the salmon steaks,
turn the foil joins over twice to ensure
a tight seal.

RICE, NOODLES AND PASTA

You don't need a lot of salmon to make an impact in a pasta dish. Penne with Cream and Smoked Salmon, for instance, uses just a few slices of smoked salmon, but when the slices are cut into strips and tossed with cream, pasta, butter and fresh thyme, the results are superb. Salmon is very good with rice, too, whether as a classic risotto, in Creamy Fish Pilau or as the basis of that popular all-in-one dish, Salmon and Rice Gratin.

CREAMY FISH PILAU

THIS SALMON DISH IS FUSION FOOD AT ITS MOST EXCITING — THE METHOD COMES FROM INDIA AND USES THAT COUNTRY'S BASMATI RICE, BUT THE WINE AND CREAM SAUCE IS FRENCH IN FLAVOUR.

SERVES 4–6

INGREDIENTS
    450g/1lb fresh mussels, scrubbed
    350ml/12fl oz/1½ cups white wine
    fresh flat leaf parsley sprig
    about 675g/1½lb salmon
    225g/8oz scallops
    about 15ml/1 tbsp olive oil
    40g/1½oz/3 tbsp butter
    2 shallots, finely chopped
    225g/8oz/3 cups button (white)
        mushrooms
    275g/10oz/1½ cups basmati rice,
        soaked in cold water for 30 minutes
    300ml/½ pint/1¼ cups fish stock
    150ml/¼ pint/⅔ cup double
        (heavy) cream
    15ml/1 tbsp chopped fresh parsley
    225g/8oz large cooked prawns
        (shrimp), peeled and deveined
    salt and ground black pepper
    fresh flat leaf parsley sprigs,
        to garnish

1 Preheat the oven to 160°C/325°F/ Gas 3. Place the mussels in a pan with 90ml/6 tbsp of the wine and the parsley. Cover and cook for 4–5 minutes until the mussels have opened. Drain, reserving the cooking liquid. Remove the mussels from their shells, discarding any that have not opened.

2 Cut the salmon into bitesize pieces. Detach the corals from the scallops and cut the white scallop flesh into thick pieces of equal width.

3 Heat half the oil and all the butter and fry the shallots and mushrooms for 3–4 minutes. Transfer to a bowl. Heat the remaining oil and fry the rice for 2–3 minutes. Spoon into a casserole.

4 Pour the stock, remaining wine and reserved mussel liquid into a frying pan, and bring to the boil. Off the heat, stir in the cream and parsley. Season lightly. Pour over the rice, then add the salmon and the scallop flesh, together with the mushroom mixture. Stir carefully to mix.

5 Cover the casserole tightly. Bake for 30–35 minutes, then add the scallop corals, replace the cover and cook for 4 minutes more. Add the mussels and prawns, cover and cook for 3–4 minutes until the seafood is heated through and the rice is tender. Serve garnished with the parsley sprigs.

SALMON AND RICE GRATIN

THIS ALL-IN-ONE SUPPER DISH IS IDEAL FOR INFORMAL ENTERTAINING AS IT CAN BE MADE AHEAD OF TIME AND REHEATED FOR ABOUT HALF AN HOUR BEFORE BEING SERVED WITH A TOSSED SALAD.

SERVES 6

INGREDIENTS
  675g/1½lb fresh salmon fillet, skinned
  1 bay leaf
  a few parsley stalks
  1 litre/1¾ pints/4 cups water
  400g/14oz/2 cups basmati rice,
    soaked in cold water for 30 minutes
  30–45ml/2–3 tbsp chopped fresh
    parsley, plus extra to garnish
  175g/6oz/1½ cups grated
    Cheddar cheese
  3 hard-boiled eggs, chopped
  salt and ground black pepper

For the sauce
  1 litre/1¾ pints/4 cups milk
  40g/1½oz/⅓ cup plain
    (all-purpose) flour
  40g/1½oz/3 tbsp butter
  5ml/1 tsp mild curry paste or
    Dijon mustard

1 Put the salmon in a wide, shallow pan. Add the bay leaf and parsley stalks, with salt and pepper. Pour in the water and bring to simmering point. Poach the fish for about 12 minutes until just tender.

2 Lift the fish out of the pan using a slotted spoon, then strain the liquid into a clean pan. Leave the fish to cool, then remove any visible bones and flake the flesh gently with a fork.

3 Drain the rice and add it to the pan containing the fish-poaching liquid. Bring to the boil, then reduce the heat, cover and simmer for 10 minutes.

4 Remove the pan from the heat and, without lifting the lid, allow the rice to stand undisturbed for 5 minutes.

5 Meanwhile, make the sauce. Mix the milk, flour and butter in a pan. Bring to the boil over a low heat, whisking constantly until the sauce is smooth and thick. Stir in the curry paste or mustard, with salt and pepper to taste. Reduce the heat and simmer the sauce for 2 minutes, whisking occasionally.

6 Preheat the grill (broiler). Remove the sauce from the heat and stir in the chopped parsley and rice, with half the cheese. Using a large metal spoon, fold in the flaked fish and eggs.

7 Spoon into a shallow gratin dish and sprinkle with the rest of the cheese. Heat under the grill until the topping is golden brown and bubbling. Serve in individual dishes, garnished with chopped parsley.

SALMON RISOTTO WITH CUCUMBER

THIS SIMPLE RISOTTO IS COOKED ALL IN ONE GO, AND IS THEREFORE EASIER TO MAKE THAN THE
USUAL RISOTTO. NEVERTHELESS, IT IS VERY CREAMY AND THE SALMON GIVES IT SUPERB FLAVOUR.

SERVES 4

INGREDIENTS
  25g/1oz/2 tbsp butter
  small bunch of spring onions
    (scallions), white parts only, chopped
  ½ cucumber, peeled, seeded
    and chopped
  350g/12oz/1¾ cups risotto rice
  1.2 litres/2 pints/5 cups hot fish or
    chicken stock
  150ml/¼ pint/⅔ cup dry white wine
  450g/1lb salmon fillet, skinned
    and diced
  45ml/3 tbsp chopped fresh tarragon
  salt and ground black pepper

3 Stir in the diced salmon and then
season. Continue cooking for a further
5 minutes, stirring occasionally, then
switch off the heat. Cover the pan and
leave the risotto to stand for 5 minutes.

4 Remove the lid from the pan, add the
chopped tarragon to the rice and mix
lightly. Spoon into a warmed bowl and
serve. Offer extra chopped tarragon on
the side, if you like.

1 Heat the butter and cook the spring
onions and cucumber. Cook for 2
minutes without letting the onions brown.

2 Stir in the rice, then pour in the stock
and wine. Bring to the boil, then lower
the heat and simmer, uncovered, for
10 minutes, stirring occasionally.

VARIATION
Carnaroli rice would be excellent in this
risotto, although if it is not available,
arborio rice can be used instead.

STIR-FRIED NOODLES <u>WITH</u> SOY SALMON

TERIYAKI SAUCE FORMS THE MARINADE FOR THE SALMON IN THIS RECIPE. SERVED WITH SOFT-FRIED NOODLES, IT MAKES A STUNNING DISH.

<u>SERVES 4</u>

INGREDIENTS

    350g/12oz salmon fillet,
      skinned
    30ml/2 tbsp shoyu (Japanese
      soy sauce)
    30ml/2 tbsp sake
    60ml/4 tbsp mirin or sweet sherry
    5ml/1 tsp soft light brown sugar
    10ml/2 tsp grated fresh root ginger
    3 garlic cloves, 1 crushed, and 2
      sliced into rounds
    30ml/2 tbsp groundnut
      (peanut) oil
    225g/8oz dried egg noodles, cooked
      and drained
    50g/2oz/1 cup alfalfa sprouts
    30ml/2 tbsp sesame seeds,
      lightly toasted

1 Using a sharp cook's knife, slice the salmon thinly. Spread out the slices in a large, shallow dish, keeping them in a single layer if possible.

2 In a bowl, mix together the soy sauce, sake, mirin or sherry, sugar, ginger and crushed garlic. Pour over the salmon, cover and leave for 30 minutes.

3 Preheat the grill (broiler). Drain the salmon, reserving the marinade. Place the salmon in a layer on a baking sheet. Cook under the grill for 2–3 minutes.

4 Meanwhile, heat a wok until hot, add the oil and swirl it around. Add the garlic rounds and cook until golden brown. Remove the garlic and discard.

5 Add the cooked noodles and reserved marinade to the wok and stir-fry for 3–4 minutes until the marinade has reduced to a syrupy glaze and coats the noodles.

6 Toss in the alfalfa sprouts. Transfer immediately to warmed serving plates and top with the salmon. Sprinkle over the toasted sesame seeds. Serve at once.

PENNE WITH CREAM AND SMOKED SALMON

NO SUPPER DISH COULD BE SIMPLER. FRESHLY COOKED PASTA IS TOSSED WITH CREAM, SMOKED SALMON AND THYME. FROM START TO FINISH IT TAKES UNDER 15 MINUTES TO MAKE.

SERVES 4

INGREDIENTS
  350g/12oz/3 cups dried penne
  115g/4oz thinly sliced
    smoked salmon
  2–3 fresh thyme sprigs
  25g/1oz/2 tbsp butter
  150ml/¼ pint/⅔ cup double
    (heavy) cream
  salt and ground black pepper

VARIATION
Substitute low fat cream cheese for half the cream in the sauce, for a less rich mixture that still tastes very good.

1 Bring a large pan of lightly salted water to the boil. Add the pasta and cook for about 12 minutes, or according to the instructions on the packet, until the penne are tender but still firm to the bite.

2 Meanwhile, using kitchen scissors or a small, sharp knife, cut the smoked salmon into thin strips, each about 5mm/¼in wide, and place on a plate. Strip the leaves from the thyme sprigs.

3 Melt the butter in a large pan. Stir in the cream with a quarter of the salmon and thyme leaves, then season with pepper. Heat gently for 3–4 minutes, stirring constantly. Do not allow the sauce to boil. Taste for seasoning.

4 Drain the pasta, return it to the pan, and toss it in the cream and salmon sauce. Divide among four warmed bowls and top with the remaining salmon and thyme leaves. Serve immediately.

SPAGHETTI WITH SALMON AND PRAWNS

THIS IS A LOVELY, FRESH-TASTING PASTA DISH, PERFECT FOR AN AL-FRESCO MEAL IN SUMMER. SERVE IT AS A MAIN COURSE LUNCH WITH WARM ITALIAN BREAD AND A DRY WHITE WINE.

SERVES 4

INGREDIENTS
300g/11oz salmon fillet
200ml/7fl oz/scant 1 cup dry
  white wine
a few fresh basil sprigs, plus extra
  basil leaves, to garnish
6 ripe Italian plum tomatoes,
  peeled and finely chopped
150ml/¼ pint/⅔ cup double
  (heavy) cream
350g/12oz/3 cups fresh or
  dried spaghetti
115g/4oz/⅔ cup peeled cooked
  prawns (shrimp), thawed and
  thoroughly dried if frozen
salt and ground black pepper

COOK'S TIP
Check the salmon fillet carefully for small bones when you are flaking the flesh. Although the salmon is already filleted, you will always find a few stray "pin" bones. Pick them out carefully using tweezers or your fingertips.

1 Put the salmon, skin side up, in a wide shallow pan. Pour over the wine, then add the basil. Sprinkle the fish with salt and pepper. Bring the wine to the boil, cover the pan and simmer gently for 5 minutes. Lift the fish out of the pan and set it aside to cool a little.

2 Add the tomatoes and cream to the liquid remaining in the pan and bring to the boil. Stir well, then reduce the heat and simmer, uncovered, for 10–15 minutes. Meanwhile, cook the pasta according to the instructions on the packet.

3 Flake the fish into large chunks, discarding the skin and any bones. Add the fish to the sauce with the prawns, shaking the pan until they are well coated. Taste the sauce for seasoning.

4 Drain the pasta and put it in a warmed bowl. Pour the sauce over the pasta and toss to combine. Serve immediately, garnished with fresh basil leaves.

PASTA WITH SMOKED SALMON

*THIS IS A PRETTY PASTA DISH THAT TASTES AS GOOD AS IT LOOKS.
THE LIGHT TEXTURE OF THE CUCUMBER PERFECTLY COMPLEMENTS
THE SMOKED SALMON AND THE PASTEL COLOURS LOOK VERY
ATTRACTIVE AGAINST THE CREAMY SWIRLS OF TAGLIATELLE.*

SERVES 4

INGREDIENTS
    350g/12oz/3 cups dried or
      fresh tagliatelle
    ½ cucumber
    75g/3oz/6 tbsp butter
    grated rind of 1 orange
    30ml/2 tbsp chopped fresh dill
    300ml/½ pint/1¼ cups single
      (light) cream
    15ml/1 tbsp orange juice
    115g/4oz smoked salmon, skinned
    salt and ground black pepper

1 Bring a large pan of lightly salted
water to the boil and add the pasta. If
using dried pasta, cook for about 12
minutes or for the time recommended
on the packet. If using fresh pasta,
cook for 2–3 minutes, or until just
tender but still firm to the bite.

3 Melt the butter in a heavy pan, add
the grated orange rind and fresh dill
and stir well. Add the cucumber
and cook over a low heat for about
2 minutes, stirring from time to time
with a wooden spoon.

4 Stir in the cream and orange juice,
with salt and pepper to taste. Reduce
the heat to the lowest setting and cook
gently for 1 minute.

2 Using a sharp knife, cut the
cucumber in half lengthways, then
use a small spoon to scoop out and
discard the cucumber seeds. Turn
the cucumber on to the flat side and
slice it thinly in crescent shapes.

5 Cut the salmon into thin strips. Stir
these into the sauce and heat through.

6 Drain the pasta thoroughly and
return it to the pan. Add the sauce
and toss to combine. Spoon into a
dish or into individual shallow pasta
plates and serve.

COOK'S TIP
If the cost of smoked salmon deters you
from using it too often, consider buying
salmon pieces or off-cuts. These aren't
inferior in any way, but because they are
either too small or too awkwardly shaped
to look good in a packet, they are much
cheaper than the neater slices.

SEAFOOD LASAGNE

THIS DISH CAN BE AS SIMPLE OR AS ELEGANT AS YOU LIKE. FOR A DINNER PARTY, DRESS IT UP WITH
SCALLOPS, MUSSELS OR PRAWNS AND A REALLY GENEROUS PINCH OF SAFFRON IN THE SAUCE; FOR A
FAMILY SUPPER, USE SIMPLE FISH SUCH AS COD AND SMOKED HADDOCK.

SERVES 8

INGREDIENTS
    350g/12oz monkfish
    350g/12oz salmon fillet
    350g/12oz undyed smoked haddock
    1 litre/1¾ pints/4 cups milk
    500ml/17fl oz/2¼ cups fish stock
    2 bay leaves or a good pinch of
      saffron threads
    1 small onion, halved
    75g/3oz/6 tbsp butter, plus extra
      for greasing
    45ml/3 tbsp plain (all-purpose) flour
    150g/5oz/2 cups mushrooms,
      sliced
    225–300g/8–11oz no pre-cook or
      fresh lasagne
    60ml/4 tbsp freshly grated
      Parmesan cheese
    salt, ground black pepper, grated
      nutmeg and paprika
    rocket (arugula) leaves,
      to garnish

For the tomato sauce
    30ml/2 tbsp olive oil
    1 red onion, finely chopped
    1 garlic clove, finely chopped
    400g/14oz can chopped tomatoes
    15ml/1 tbsp tomato purée (paste)
    15ml/1 tbsp torn fresh basil leaves

2 Put all the fish in a shallow flameproof dish or pan with the milk, stock, bay leaves or saffron and onion. Bring to the boil over a medium heat; poach for 5 minutes, until almost cooked.

3 When the fish is almost cold, lift it out of the pan and place on a board. Strain the liquid and reserve it. Remove skin and any bones, then flake the fish.

1 Make the tomato sauce. Heat the oil in a pan and fry the onion and garlic over a low heat for 5 minutes, until softened and golden. Stir in the tomatoes and tomato purée and simmer for 20–30 minutes, stirring occasionally. Season and stir in the basil.

4 Preheat the oven to 180°C/350°F/ Gas 4. Melt the butter in a pan and stir in the flour. Cook for 2 minutes, stirring. Gradually add the poaching liquid and bring to the boil, stirring. Stir in the mushrooms. Cook for 2–3 minutes, then season with salt, pepper and nutmeg.

5 Lightly grease a shallow ovenproof dish. Spoon a thin layer of the mushroom sauce over the base of the dish and spread it with a spatula. Stir the fish into the remaining mushroom sauce in the pan.

6 Make a layer of lasagne, then a layer of fish and sauce. Add another layer of lasagne, then spread over all the tomato sauce. Continue to layer the lasagne and fish, finishing with a layer of fish and sauce.

7 Sprinkle over the grated Parmesan cheese. Bake for 30–45 minutes, until bubbling and golden. Remove from the oven and leave to stand for 10 minutes. Sprinkle with paprika. Garnish with rocket leaves and serve.

COOK'S TIP
Use fresh lasagne, if available. Cook the sheets in a large pan of lightly salted boiling water for 3 minutes. Do not overcrowd the pan or the sheets will stick together.

FARFALLE WITH SMOKED SALMON AND DILL

THIS QUICK, LUXURIOUS SAUCE FOR PASTA HAS BECOME VERY FASHIONABLE IN ITALY, BUT WHEREVER YOU HAVE IT, IT WILL TASTE DELICIOUS. DILL IS THE CLASSIC HERB FOR COOKING WITH FISH, BUT IF YOU DON'T LIKE ITS ANISEED FLAVOUR, SUBSTITUTE PARSLEY OR A LITTLE FRESH TARRAGON.

SERVES 4

INGREDIENTS

6 spring onions (scallions), sliced
50g/2oz/¼ cup butter
90ml/6 tbsp dry white wine
  or vermouth
450ml/¾ pint/scant 2 cups double
  (heavy) cream
freshly grated nutmeg
225g/8oz smoked salmon
30ml/2 tbsp chopped fresh dill
freshly squeezed lemon juice
450g/1lb/4 cups farfalle
salt and ground black pepper
fresh dill sprigs, to garnish

1 Using a sharp cook's knife, slice the spring onions finely. Melt the butter in a large pan and fry the spring onions for about 1 minute, stirring occasionally, until softened.

2 Add the wine or vermouth and boil hard to reduce to about 30ml/2 tbsp. Stir in the cream and add salt, pepper and nutmeg to taste. Bring to the boil, then simmer for 2–3 minutes until slightly thickened.

3 Cut the smoked salmon slices into 2.5cm/1in squares and stir into the sauce, together with the dill. Add a little lemon juice to taste. Keep warm.

4 Cook the pasta in a large pan of boiling salted water, following the instructions on the packet. Drain well. Toss with the sauce. Spoon into serving bowls and serve immediately, garnished with sprigs of dill.

CREAMY LEMON AND SALMON PAPPARDELLE

THIS IS A FANTASTIC ALL-IN-ONE SUPPER DISH THAT TASTES GREAT AND IS MADE IN JUST A FEW MINUTES — IDEAL FOR WHEN YOU'RE REALLY HUNGRY BUT HAVEN'T MUCH TIME. SERVE IT WITH A ROCKET SALAD DRESSED WITH EXTRA VIRGIN OLIVE OIL, BALSAMIC VINEGAR AND BLACK PEPPER.

SERVES 4

INGREDIENTS
    500g/1¼lb fresh pappardelle or
        tagliatelle
    300ml/½ pint/1¼ cups single
        (light) cream
    grated rind and juice of 2 lemons
    225g/8oz smoked salmon pieces
    2.5ml/½ tsp grated nutmeg
    60ml/4 tbsp chopped fresh parsley
    salt and ground black pepper
    Parmesan cheese shavings, to garnish
    rocket (arugula) salad, to serve

1 Bring a large pan of lightly salted water to the boil and cook the pappardelle or tagliatelle for 3–5 minutes, or according to the instructions on the packet, until risen to the surface of the boiling water and just tender. Drain well.

2 Add the cream, lemon rind and juice to the pan and heat through gently until piping hot. Return the cooked pappardelle to the pan and stir thoroughly to coat the pasta with the creamy mixture.

3 Add the salmon pieces, grated nutmeg, chopped parsley and plenty of ground black pepper to the sauce in the pan and stir well to combine.

4 Divide the pasta among four warmed serving plates and top with the Parmesan shavings. Serve immediately with the rocket salad.

LIGHT AND HEALTHY

Low in calories, but high in the essential fatty acids that are vital for good health, salmon is an important ingredient in a healthy diet. That doesn't mean, however, that all the recipes in this book are tailored to those who are trying to trim their weight. Elsewhere you'll find cream sauces, pastry and flavoured butters, but in this chapter the emphasis is on sensible eating. Dishes include Haddock and Smoked Salmon Terrine, Rice Cakes with Smoked Salmon, and Marinated Salmon with Avocado — delicious but without a hint of self-denial.

HADDOCK AND SMOKED SALMON TERRINE

*THIS SUBSTANTIAL TERRINE MAKES A SUPERB DISH FOR A SUMMER BUFFET, ACCOMPANIED BY DILL
MAYONNAISE OR A FRESH MANGO SALSA.*

SERVES 6–8

INGREDIENTS

- 15ml/1 tbsp sunflower oil,
  for greasing
- 350g/12oz oak-smoked salmon
- 900g/2lb haddock fillets, skinned
- 2 eggs, lightly beaten
- 105ml/7 tbsp low-fat crème fraîche
  or sour cream
- 30ml/2 tbsp drained bottled capers
- 30ml/2 tbsp drained soft green or
  pink peppercorns
- salt and ground white pepper
- low-fat crème fraîche or sour cream,
  peppercorns and fresh dill and
  rocket (arugula), to garnish

3 Combine the eggs, crème fraîche or sour cream, capers and soft peppercorns in a bowl. Season with salt and white pepper, then stir in the small pieces of haddock. Spoon half the mixture into the mould. Smooth the surface with a spatula.

6 Tap the terrine to settle the contents, then stand it in a roasting pan and pour in boiling water to come halfway up the sides of the terrine. Place in the oven and cook for 45 minutes–1 hour, until the filling is just set.

1 Preheat the oven to 200°C/400°F/ Gas 6. Grease a 1 litre/1¾ pint/4 cup loaf pan or terrine. Use some of the salmon to line the pan or terrine; let some of the ends overhang the mould. Reserve the remaining smoked salmon.

4 Wrap the long haddock fillets in the reserved smoked salmon. Don't worry if there isn't enough salmon to cover them completely. Lay the wrapped haddock fillets on top of the fish mixture in the pan or terrine.

7 Take the terrine out of the roasting pan, but do not remove the foil cover. Place two or three large heavy cans on the foil to weight it and leave until cold. Chill in the refrigerator for 24 hours.

8 About 1 hour before serving, remove the terrine from the refrigerator, lift off the weights and remove the foil. Carefully invert the terrine on to a serving plate and lift off the pan or terrine.

9 Cut the terrine into thick slices, using a sharp knife. Serve, garnished with crème fraîche or sour cream, peppercorns and fronds of dill and rocket leaves.

2 Cut two long slices of haddock the length of the pan or terrine and set aside. Cut the rest of the haddock into small pieces. Season all the haddock with salt and pepper.

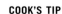

5 Fill the pan or terrine with the rest of the fish mixture, smooth the surface and fold the overhanging pieces of smoked salmon over the top. Cover tightly with a double thickness of foil.

COOK'S TIP

A perfectly clean house brick, wrapped in clear film (plastic wrap) can be used instead of the cans to weight the terrine.

EGG AND SALMON PUFF PARCELS

THESE ELEGANT PARCELS HIDE A MOUTHWATERING MIXTURE OF FLAVOURS, AND MAKE A DELICIOUS
APPETIZER OR LUNCH DISH. SERVE WITH CURRY-FLAVOURED MAYONNAISE OR HOLLANDAISE SAUCE.

SERVES 6

INGREDIENTS

75g/3oz/scant ½ cup long grain rice
300ml/½ pint/1¼ cups good-quality
  fish stock
350g/12oz tail pieces of salmon
juice of ½ lemon
15ml/1 tbsp chopped fresh dill
15ml/1 tbsp chopped fresh parsley
10ml/2 tsp mild curry powder
6 small (US medium) eggs,
  soft-boiled and cooled
425g/15oz flaky or puff pastry,
  thawed if frozen
1 egg, beaten
salt and ground black pepper

VARIATION

You could replace the hen's eggs with
quail's eggs for a luxury touch.

1 Place the rice in a large pan and cook
according to the instructions on the
packet, using fish stock instead of
water, then drain and cool. Preheat the
oven to 220°C/425°F/Gas 7.

2 Place the salmon in a large pan and
cover with cold water. Gently heat until
the water is not quite simmering and
cook the fish for 8–10 minutes until it
flakes easily when tested.

3 Lift the salmon out of the pan and
remove the bones and skin. Flake the
fish into the rice, add the lemon juice,
herbs, curry powder and seasoning, and
mix well. Peel the eggs.

4 Roll out the pastry and cut into six
15cm/6in squares. Brush the edges
with the beaten egg. Place a spoonful of
the rice mixture in the middle of each
square, push an egg into the centre and
top with a little more of the rice mixture.
Pull over the pastry corners to the
middle to form a neat, square parcel,
pressing the joins together with your
fingers firmly to seal.

5 Brush the parcels with more beaten
egg, place on a baking sheet and bake
for 20 minutes, then reduce the oven
temperature to 190°C/375°F/Gas 5.
Cook for 10 minutes more, until golden
and crisp. Cool slightly before serving.

SCRAMBLED EGGS WITH SMOKED SALMON

FOR A LUXURY BREAKFAST, OR A LATE-NIGHT SUPPER, YOU CAN'T BEAT THIS SPECIAL COMBINATION.
SERVE IT WITH BUCK'S FIZZ: CHAMPAGNE MIXED WITH FRESHLY SQUEEZED ORANGE JUICE.

<u>SERVES 4</u>

INGREDIENTS

  4 slices of pumpernickel or
    wholemeal (whole-wheat) bread,
    crusts trimmed
  50g/2oz/¼ cup butter
  115g/4oz thinly sliced smoked salmon
  6 eggs
  105ml/7 tbsp crème fraîche or sour
    cream
  salt and ground black pepper
  generous 60ml/4 tbsp salmon roe
    or lumpfish roe and sprigs of dill,
    to garnish

VARIATION

If you are lucky enough to have a truffle,
another treat is to grate a little into the
scrambled eggs. Serve them on toast,
topped with a little chopped fresh chervil.

1 Spread the slices of pumpernickel or
wholemeal bread with half of the butter
and arrange the smoked salmon on top.
Cut each slice in half, place two halves
on each serving plate and set aside
while you make the scrambled eggs.

2 Lightly beat the eggs in a bowl and
season with salt and freshly ground
pepper. Melt the remaining butter in
a pan until sizzling, then quickly stir
in the beaten eggs.

3 Stir constantly until the eggs begin to
thicken. Just before they have finished
cooking, remove the saucepan from the
heat and stir in the crème fraîche or
sour cream. Set the eggs aside and
keep warm.

4 Spoon the scrambled eggs on to
the smoked salmon. Top each serving
with a spoonful of salmon roe or
lumpfish roe and serve, garnished
with sprigs of dill.

BAKED SALMON, CZECH-STYLE

THIS CENTRAL EUROPEAN WAY OF COOKING SALMON IS VERY EASY, AND THE RESULTS ARE EXCELLENT. THE FISH COOKS IN ITS OWN JUICES, WITH CARAWAY SEEDS ADDING THEIR OWN INIMITABLE FLAVOUR.

SERVES 6

INGREDIENTS

1.8kg/4lb whole salmon, cleaned
115g/4oz/½ cup butter, melted
2.5–5ml/½–1 tsp caraway seeds
45ml/3 tbsp lemon juice
salt and ground black pepper
sprigs of flat leaf parsley and lemon
   wedges, to garnish

COOK'S TIP
Take care when slicing off the fins from the salmon as they can be sharp enough to cut fingers.

1 Preheat the oven to 180°C/350°F/ Gas 4. Scale the salmon, remove the head and tail and slice off the fins with a sharp filleting knife, then cut the fish in half lengthways.

2 Place the salmon, skin side down, in a lightly greased roasting pan. Brush with the melted butter. Season generously with salt and ground black pepper, sprinkle over the caraway seeds and drizzle with lemon juice.

3 Cover the salmon loosely with foil and bake for 25 minutes. Remove it from the oven, lift off the foil and test the fish. It is done if it is opaque and flakes easily when tested with the point of a knife. Bake for a little longer if needed.

4 Remove the foil and carefully lift the fish on to a serving plate, using two fish slices or large spatulas. Garnish with flat leaf parsley and lemon wedges. The baked salmon can be served straight away, but also tastes good cold.

RICE CAKES WITH SMOKED SALMON

THESE ELEGANT RICE CAKES ARE MADE USING A RISOTTO BASE. YOU COULD SKIP THIS STAGE AND USE LEFTOVER SEAFOOD OR MUSHROOM RISOTTO INSTEAD. A TOMATO RISOTTO WOULD ALSO WORK WELL.

SERVES 4

INGREDIENTS
    30ml/2 tbsp olive oil
    1 medium onion, chopped
    225g/8oz/generous 1 cup risotto rice
    about 90ml/6 tbsp white wine
    about 750ml/1¼ pints/3 cups fish or
      chicken stock
    15g/½oz/2 tbsp dried porcini
      mushrooms, soaked for 10 minutes
      in warm water to cover
    15ml/1 tbsp chopped fresh parsley
    15ml/1 tbsp chopped fresh chives
    5ml/1 tsp chopped fresh dill
    1 egg, lightly beaten
    about 45ml/3 tbsp ground rice, plus
      extra for dusting
    oil, for frying
    60ml/4 tbsp sour cream
    175g/6oz smoked salmon
    salt and ground black pepper
    radicchio and oakleaf salad, tossed in
      French dressing, to serve

3 Add the beaten egg, then stir in enough ground rice to bind the mixture – it should be soft but manageable. Dust your hands with ground rice and shape the mixture into four patties, each about 13cm/5in in diameter and about 2cm/¾in thick.

4 Heat the oil and fry the rice cakes for 4–5 minutes until browned on both sides. Drain and cool slightly. Place each rice cake on a plate and top with 15ml/1 tbsp sour cream. Twist two or three slices of smoked salmon on top, and serve with a dressed salad garnish.

1 Heat the olive oil in a pan and fry the onion for 3–4 minutes until soft. Add the rice and cook, stirring, until the grains are thoroughly coated in oil. Pour in the wine and stock, a little at a time, stirring constantly over a gentle heat until each quantity of liquid has been absorbed before adding more.

2 Drain the mushrooms and chop them into small pieces. When the rice is tender, and all the liquid has been absorbed, stir in the mushrooms, parsley, chives and dill, with salt and pepper to taste. Remove from the heat and set aside for a few minutes to cool.

LEMONY SALMON LOAF WITH CUCUMBER

CHOOSE CANNED RED SALMON RATHER THAN THE PINK VARIETY FOR THIS EASY ALL-IN-ONE LOAF AS THE FLAVOUR AND TEXTURE ARE MUCH IMPROVED. THIS LOAF IS IDEAL FOR PICNICS OR IT CAN BE SERVED WITH THE CUCUMBER SAUCE AS A LIGHT SUMMER LUNCH OR SUPPER DISH.

SERVES 4–6

INGREDIENTS
150ml/¼ pint/⅔ cup milk
2 eggs, beaten
115g/4oz/2 cups fresh white
  breadcrumbs
butter, for greasing
75g/3oz celery
400g/14oz can salmon, drained
grated rind and juice of 1 lemon
salt and ground black pepper
lemon slices, to garnish

For the sauce
1 cucumber, peeled, seeded
  and chopped
25g/1oz/2 tbsp butter
15ml/1 tbsp plain (all-purpose)
  flour
rind and juice of ½ lemon
1 egg yolk

1 Mix the milk, eggs and breadcrumbs in a large bowl and leave to stand for 10 minutes.

2 Preheat the oven to 180°C/350°F/ Gas 4. Grease a 450g/1lb loaf tin (pan) with butter. Chop the celery finely and set it aside.

3 Place the drained salmon in a bowl and flake with a fork. Add to the breadcrumb mixture with the chopped celery, grated lemon rind and juice. Season with salt and pepper to taste.

4 Stir the mixture until evenly blended. Pour into the prepared loaf tin and bake for 1 hour or until a skewer inserted into the centre of the loaf comes out clean. Leave the loaf in the tin to cool slightly.

5 Make the sauce. Place the cucumber pieces in a small pan, cover with cold water and simmer until just tender. Using a slotted spoon, remove the cucumber and set it aside. Pour the cooking liquid into a measuring jug (cup). Add enough water to make up the liquid to 300ml/½ pint/1¼ cups.

6 Melt the butter in the clean pan. Stir in the flour using a wooden spoon. Cook, stirring constantly, for 1 minute, then gradually add the reserved liquid, stirring until it boils and thickens.

7 Add the lemon rind and juice to the sauce in the pan, then stir in the cooked cucumber. Beat the egg yolk in a separate container and stir in a little of the hot sauce. Pour into the pan and heat gently, without boiling, until the sauce thickens a little more. Season to taste with salt and ground black pepper.

8 Using a spatula, loosen the salmon loaf from the sides of the tin and invert it on a serving dish. Garnish the loaf with lemon slices. Serve the warm cucumber sauce on the side.

VARIATION
Fennel could be used instead of the celery. It has a delicious taste and goes well with salmon. Quarter and core a fennel bulb, saving the fronds to add to the garnish for the loaf. Chop the fennel finely and toss it with the lemon juice so that it doesn't discolour.

COOK'S TIP
Lining the base of the loaf tin (pan) with non-stick baking parchment will make it easier to unmould the loaf.

SALMON <u>WITH</u> ROASTED VEGETABLES

THIS COLOURFUL AND TASTY DISH IS PERFECT FOR A SUMMER MEAL, AND BECAUSE IT IS SO EASY TO COOK, YOU DON'T HAVE TO SPEND TIME IN THE KITCHEN WHEN YOU COULD BE SOAKING UP THE SUN.

SERVES 4

INGREDIENTS

175g/6oz green beans, trimmed
1 red (bell) pepper, seeded
  and sliced
1 yellow (bell) pepper, seeded
  and sliced
16 cherry tomatoes, halved
50g/2oz/½ cup pitted
  black olives
50g/2oz/½ cup pitted
  green olives
30ml/2 tbsp garlic-flavoured olive oil
4 salmon fillets, each about
  200g/7oz
juice of ½ lemon
30ml/2 tbsp olive oil
1 bunch fresh basil, leaves stripped
  from stems
salt and ground black pepper
walnut bread and olive oil, to serve

1 Preheat the oven to 220ºC/425ºF/ Gas 7. Bring a pan of lightly salted water to the boil. Add the trimmed green beans and cook them over a medium heat until they are just tender.

2 Drain the green beans very well, then put them into a large bowl. Add the red and yellow peppers, the tomatoes and the olives. Season well, drizzle the garlic oil over and stir to coat.

3 Place the salmon fillets in a single layer in a roasting pan. Pour over the lemon juice and olive oil. Turn the salmon fillets to coat them in the mixture. Season with salt and pepper.

4 Spoon the vegetable mixture into a separate roasting pan. Set aside eight basil leaves for the garnish, and tuck the rest among the vegetables.

5 Place both roasting pans in the oven, with the vegetables on a higher shelf than the fish. Bake for about 15 minutes or until the fish is opaque and the vegetables are just beginning to char at the edges.

6 To serve, arrange the vegetables on four serving plates. Top each portion with a salmon fillet and garnish with the reserved basil leaves. Serve with walnut bread and olive oil for dipping.

VARIATION
This dish works well with any thick fish fillets – try it with tuna or cod for a change.

MARINATED SALMON WITH AVOCADO

USE ONLY THE FRESHEST OF SALMON FOR THIS DELICIOUS SALAD. THE MARINADE OF LEMON AND DASHI-KONBU "COOKS" THE SALMON, WHICH IS SERVED WITH AVOCADO, ALMONDS AND SALAD LEAVES.

2 Pour the lemon juice and put two of the dashi-konbu pieces into a wide shallow plastic container. Lay the salmon fillets in the base and sprinkle with the rest of the dashi-konbu. Marinate for 15 minutes, then turn once and leave for 15 minutes more. Drain and pat dry with kitchen paper.

3 Holding a very sharp knife at an angle, cut the salmon into 5mm/¼in thick slices against the grain.

4 Halve the avocado and brush the cut surface with a little of the remaining salmon marinade. Remove the avocado stone (pit) and skin, then carefully slice to the same thickness as the salmon.

SERVES 4

INGREDIENTS
    250g/9oz very fresh salmon tail,
      skinned and filleted
    juice of 1 lemon
    10cm/4in dashi-konbu (dried kelp
      seaweed), wiped with a damp cloth
      and cut into 4 strips
    1 ripe avocado
    4 shiso leaves, stalks removed and
      cut in half lengthways
    about 115g/4oz mixed leaves such
      as lamb's lettuce, frisée or rocket
      (arugula)
    45ml/3 tbsp flaked or sliced almonds,
      toasted in a dry frying pan

For the miso mayonnaise
    90ml/6 tbsp good-quality mayonnaise
    15ml/1 tbsp shiro miso
    ground black pepper
    15ml/1 tbsp lemon juice

1 Cut the first salmon fillet in half crossways at the tail end where the fillet is not wider than 4cm/1½in. Next, cut the wider part in half lengthways. This means the fillet from one side is cut into three. Cut the other fillet into three pieces in the same way.

COOK'S TIP
Shiro miso, fermented soya bean paste, can be bought at Japanese food stores.

5 Make miso mayonnaise by mixing the mayonnaise, shiro miso and pepper in a small bowl. Spread about 5ml/1 tsp on to the back of each of the shiso leaves, then mix the remainder with the lemon juice to loosen the mayonnaise.

6 Arrange the salad on four plates. Top with the avocado, salmon, shiso leaves and almonds. Drizzle over the remaining miso mayonnaise. Serve immediately.

SALMON AND VEGETABLES IN A PARCEL

FOR THIS DELIGHTFUL JAPANESE RECIPE, SALMON IS STEAMED WITH SAKE AND BEAUTIFULLY CARVED VEGETABLES IN A FOIL PARCEL. WHEN THE PARCELS ARE OPENED, THE CONTENTS LOOK LOVELY.

SERVES 4

INGREDIENTS
- 500g/1¼lb salmon fillet, skinned
- 30ml/2 tbsp sake
- 15ml/1 tbsp shoyu (Japanese soy sauce), plus extra to serve (optional)
- about 250g/9oz/3 cups fresh shimeji mushrooms
- 8 fresh shiitake mushrooms
- 2.5cm/1in piece of carrot
- 4 spring onions (scallions)
- 115g/4oz/1 cup mangetouts (snow peas)
- salt

1 Preheat the oven to 190ºC/375ºF/ Gas 5. Cut the salmon into bitesize pieces. Place in a shallow bowl and add the sake and shoyu. Marinate for about 15 minutes. Drain and reserve the marinade.

2 Clean the shimeji mushrooms and chop off the hard root from each. Remove and discard the stalks from the shiitake. Carve a shallow slit on the top of each shiitake with a sharp knife inserted at a slant. Repeat from the other side to cut out a notch about 4cm/1½in long. Rotate the shiitake 90º and carve another notch to make a small white cross in the brown top.

3 Slice the carrot very thinly, then use a Japanese vegetable cutter or sharp knife to cut out 8–12 maple-leaf or flower shapes. Carefully slice the spring onions in half lengthways with a sharp knife. Trim the mangetouts.

4 Cut four sheets of foil, each about 29 x 21cm/11½ x 8½in. With the long side of one sheet facing you, arrange the salmon and shimeji mushrooms in the centre, then place a spring onion diagonally across them. Put two shiitake on top, three or four mangetouts in a fan shape and then sprinkle with a few carrot shapes.

5 Sprinkle the marinade and a good pinch of salt over the top. Fold the two longer sides of the foil together, then fold the shorter sides to seal. Repeat to make four parcels.

6 Place the parcels on a baking sheet and bake for 15–20 minutes in the middle of the preheated oven. When the foil has expanded into a balloon, the dish is ready to serve. Take the parcels to the table unopened and offer a little extra shoyu, if required.

MOOLI LAYERED ᵂᴵᵀᴴ SMOKED SALMON

THIS TRADITIONAL JAPANESE RECIPE ORIGINALLY CALLED FOR SALTED SLICED SALMON AND MOOLI TO BE PICKLED IN A WOODEN BARREL FOR A LONG TIME. THIS VERSION IS LESS SALTY AND FAR QUICKER.

1 Slice the mooli very thinly into rounds. Put in a shallow container, sprinkle with salt and vinegar, and add the chopped dashi-konbu. Mix and rub gently with your hands. Cover and leave in the refrigerator for 1 hour.

2 Drain in a sieve and squeeze out the excess liquid. If necessary, rinse with running water for 30 seconds, then drain and squeeze out again.

3 Cut the smoked salmon slices into 4cm/1½in squares. Take one slice of mooli, top with a salmon slice, then cover with another mooli slice. Repeat until all the salmon is used. Place in a shallow container, cover with clear film (plastic wrap), then leave to pickle at room temperature for up to 1 day.

4 Arrange the mooli rounds on a serving plate and put a pinch of poppy seeds in the centre.

SERVES 4

INGREDIENTS
   10cm/4in mooli (daikon), about
     6cm/2½in in diameter, peeled
   10ml/2 tsp salt
   5ml/1 tsp rice vinegar
   5cm/2in square dashi-konbu (dried
     kelp seaweed), chopped into
     1cm/½in strips
   50g/2oz smoked salmon, thinly sliced
   2.5ml/½ tsp white poppy seeds

COOK'S TIPS
• Use a good quality smoked salmon for this recipe as the flavour of cheaper varieties is often obscured, if not lost altogether, by the smoking process. The salmon must also be absolutely fresh.
• Nowadays mooli is available from most large supermarkets, but look in Japanese food stores and markets if you have difficulty finding it.
• You can use a mandoline, a food cutter or a vegetable slicer to make paper-thin slices of mooli.
• Taste the mooli after salting and squeezing to check whether it needs to be rinsed. The degree of saltiness will depend on its original water content.

SALMON TERIYAKI

SAKE TERIYAKI IS A WELL-KNOWN JAPANESE DISH, WHICH USES A SWEET AND SHINY SAUCE FOR MARINATING AS WELL AS FOR GLAZING THE INGREDIENTS.

SERVES 4

INGREDIENTS
   4 small salmon fillets with skin on,
      each weighing about 150g/5oz
   50g/2oz/1 cup beansprouts, washed
   50g/2oz mangetouts (snow peas)
   20g/³⁄₄oz carrot, cut into thin strips
   salt

For the teriyaki sauce
   45ml/3 tbsp shoyu (Japanese soy sauce)
   45ml/3 tbsp sake
   45ml/3 tbsp mirin or sweet sherry
   15ml/1 tbsp plus 10ml/2 tsp caster
      (superfine) sugar

1 Make the teriyaki sauce. Mix the shoyu, sake, mirin and 15ml/1 tbsp caster sugar in a pan. Heat, stirring, to dissolve the sugar. Cool for 1 hour.

2 Place the salmon fillets, skin side down, in a shallow glass or china dish. Pour over the teriyaki sauce. Leave to marinate for 30 minutes.

3 Meanwhile, bring a pan of lightly salted water to the boil. Add the beansprouts, then after 1 minute, the mangetouts. Leave for 1 minute then add the thin carrot strips. Remove the pan from the heat after 1 minute, then drain the vegetables and keep warm.

4 Preheat the grill (broiler) to medium. Take the salmon fillet out of the sauce and pat dry with kitchen paper. Reserve the sauce. Lightly oil a grilling (broiling) tray. Grill (broil) the salmon for about 6 minutes, turning once, until golden.

5 Meanwhile, pour the remaining teriyaki sauce into a small pan, add the remaining sugar and heat until dissolved. Brush the salmon with the sauce.

6 Continue to grill the salmon until the surface of the fish bubbles. Turn over and repeat on the other side.

7 Heap the vegetables on to serving plates. Place the salmon on top and spoon over the rest of the sauce.

COOK'S TIP
To save time, you could use ready-made teriyaki sauce for the marinade. This useful ingredient comes in bottles and is handy for marinating chicken before cooking it on the barbecue. Add a splash of sake, if you have some.

COMPRESSED SUSHI <u>WITH</u> SMOKED SALMON

THIS SIMPLE RECIPE OF VINEGARED RICE WITH SMOKED SALMON IS AN EXCELLENT INTRODUCTION TO THE ANCIENT ART OF SUSHI AND IS IDEAL FOR ANYONE NERVOUS ABOUT EATING RAW FISH.

MAKES ABOUT 12

INGREDIENTS
    200g/7oz/1 cup Japanese short grain
        rice, soaked for 20 minutes in water
        to cover
    250ml/8fl oz/1 cup water
    40ml/8 tsp rice vinegar, plus extra
        for moulding
    20ml/4 tsp caster (superfine) sugar
    5ml/1 tsp salt
    175g/6oz smoked salmon,
        thickly sliced
    15ml/1 tbsp sake
    15ml/1 tbsp water
    30ml/2 tbsp shoyu (Japanese
        soy sauce)
    1 lemon, thinly sliced into 6 x
        3mm/⅛in rings

1 Drain the rice, then put it in a pan with the measured water. Bring to the boil, then reduce the heat, cover and simmer for 20 minutes, until all the water has been absorbed. Meanwhile, heat the vinegar, sugar and salt in a pan, stir well and cool. Fold into the hot rice, then remove from the heat, cover and leave to stand for 20 minutes.

2 Lay the smoked salmon on a chopping board and sprinkle with a mixture of the sake, water and shoyu. Leave to marinate for 1 hour, then wipe dry with kitchen paper.

3 Wet a wooden Japanese sushi mould or line a 25 x 7.5 x 5cm/10 x 3 x 2in plastic container with a large sheet of clear film (plastic wrap), allowing the edges to hang over.

4 Spread half the smoked salmon to evenly cover the bottom of the mould or container. Add one-quarter of the cooked rice and firmly press down with hands dampened with rice vinegar to make a layer 1cm/½in thick. Add the remainder of the salmon, and press the remaining rice on top.

5 Put the wet wooden lid on the mould, or cover the plastic container with the overhanging clear film. Place a weight, such as a heavy dinner plate, on top. Leave in a cool place overnight, or for at least 3 hours. If you use the refrigerator, place the mould in the least cool part, such as on the top shelf.

6 Remove the compressed sushi from the mould or container and unwrap. Cut into 2cm/¾in slices and serve on a Japanese lacquered tray or a large plate. Quarter the lemon rings. Garnish each piece of sushi with two pieces of lemon and serve.

HAND-MOULDED SUSHI

IF YOU HAVE ACCESS TO QUALITY SEAFOOD AT THE PEAK OF FRESHNESS, THIS IS A WONDERFUL WAY OF APPRECIATING ITS SUPERB NATURAL FLAVOUR.

SERVES 4

INGREDIENTS
   400g/14oz/2 cups Japanese short
      grain rice, soaked for 20 minutes
      in water to cover
   500ml/18fl oz/2½ cups water
   55ml/3½ tbsp rice vinegar, plus
      extra for moulding
   30ml/2 tbsp caster (superfine) sugar
   10ml/2 tsp salt
   4 raw king prawns (jumbo shrimp),
      head and shell removed, tails intact
   4 scallops, white muscle only
   425g/15oz assorted very fresh fish,
      such as salmon, tuna, sea bass
      and mackerel, skinned, cleaned
      and filleted
   45ml/3 tbsp wasabi paste from
      a tube, or the same amount of
      wasabi powder mixed with 15ml/
      1 tbsp water
   pickled ginger, to garnish
   shoyu (Japanese soy sauce), to serve

COOK'S TIP
For moulding the vinegared rice, wet
your fingers frequently, by dipping
them in a bowl containing a mixture
of 150ml/¼ pint/⅔ cup water and
15ml/1 tbsp rice vinegar.

1 Drain the rice, then put it in a pan
with the measured water. Bring to the
boil, then reduce the heat, cover and
simmer for 20 minutes, until all the
water has been absorbed. Meanwhile,
heat the vinegar, sugar and salt in a
pan, stir well and cool. Fold into the
hot rice, then remove the pan from
the heat, cover and leave to stand for
20 minutes.

2 Insert a bamboo skewer or cocktail
stick (toothpick) into each prawn
lengthways. This stops the prawns
curling up when cooked. Boil them in
lightly salted water for 2 minutes, or
until they turn pink. Drain and cool,
then pull out the skewers. Cut open
from the belly side but do not slice in
two. With the point of a sharp knife,
remove the black vein running down
the back. Open each prawn out flat
and place on a tray.

3 Slice the scallops horizontally in half,
but not quite through. Gently open each
scallop at this "hinge" to make a
butterfly shape. Place on the tray, cut
side down. Use a sharp knife to cut all
the fish fillets into 7.5 x 4cm/3 x 1½in
pieces, 5mm/¼in thick. Place all the
raw fish and shellfish on the tray, cover
with clear film (plastic wrap), then chill
in the refrigerator for at least 1 hour, or
up to 4 hours.

4 Spoon the vinegared rice into a bowl.
Have ready a small bowl filled with
water acidulated with rice vinegar for
moulding (see Cook's Tip). Take the tray
of seafood from the refrigerator.

5 Wet your hand with the vinegared
water and scoop about 25ml/1½ tbsp
vinegared rice into your palm. Gently
but firmly grip it to make a rectangular
block. Do not squash the rice, but
ensure that the grains stick together.
The size of the blocks must be smaller
than the toppings.

6 Put the rice block on a damp
chopping board. Taking a piece of
salmon topping in your palm, rub a little
wasabi paste in the middle of it. Put the
rice block on top of the salmon and
gently press it. Form your palm into a
cup and shape the topped rice to a
smooth-surfaced mound. Place it on a
serving tray. Work quickly, or the
warmth of your hands may cause the
salmon to lose its freshness.

7 Repeat this process until all of the
rice and toppings are used. Serve
immediately with a little shoyu dribbled
on individual plates. To eat, pick up a
hand-moulded sushi and dip the tip
into the shoyu. Eat a little pickled
ginger between tasting different sushi
to refresh your mouth and prepare
yourself for a new flavour sensation.

ON THE GRILL

Anglers swear the best place to eat salmon is in the open air, and if these superb recipes are anything to go by, they are probably right. All the recipes in this chapter are cooked either on the barbecue or under the grill, so that they can be enjoyed outdoors. As the sun goes down, tuck into Salmon Kebabs with Coconut or Grilled Butterflied Salmon, or sit on the patio and sample Salmon with Spicy Pesto. Oily fish can be smoked in a kettle barbecue. If you have one of these, you've a treat in store when you tuck into Hot Smoked Salmon.

SALMON KEBABS WITH COCONUT

INSPIRED BY FLAVOURS FROM THE WEST INDIES, THIS RECIPE COMBINES COCONUT AND LIME TO PROVIDE A COUNTERPOINT TO THE SUBTLE TASTE OF SALMON AND SCALLOPS.

SERVES 6

INGREDIENTS
  450g/1lb salmon fillet, skinned
  1 small fresh coconut
  2 limes
  12 scallops
  45ml/3 tbsp freshly squeezed
    lime juice
  30ml/2 tbsp soy sauce
  30ml/2 tbsp clear honey
  15ml/1 tbsp soft light brown sugar
  ground black pepper

1 Using a sharp knife, cut the salmon into bitesize chunks and place these in a shallow bowl.

2 Halve the coconut and pour the liquor into a jug (pitcher). Using a small, sharp knife, remove the coconut flesh from the inside of the shell and cut it into chunks, making them about the same size as the salmon.

3 Cut each lime into six thick slices. Thread the coconut, salmon, scallops and pieces of lime alternately on to six skewers.

4 Add the lime juice, soy sauce, honey and sugar to the coconut liquor to make the marinade. Mix well and stir in some pepper. You will probably not need salt with the soy sauce.

5 Place the prepared kebabs in a single layer in a shallow non-metallic dish. Pour the marinade over. Cover and chill for at least 3 hours.

6 Preheat the grill (broiler) to high. Remove the kebabs from the marinade and place on the grill pan. Grill (broil) for 4 minutes on each side, turning once and basting occasionally with the marinade.

COOK'S TIP
The easiest way to open a coconut is to hold it in the palm of your left hand, with the "eyes" just above your thumb. The fault line lies between the eyes. Hold the coconut over a bowl to catch the liquid, then carefully hit the line with the blunt side of a cleaver or hammer. If you do this correctly, the coconut will split neatly into two halves.

GRILLED BUTTERFLIED SALMON

ASK YOUR FISHMONGER TO BONE THE SALMON FOR BUTTERFLYING. IF YOU ORDER THE FISH IN ADVANCE, AND GIVE THE SUPPLIER PLENTY OF TIME, MOST WILL BE HAPPY TO OBLIGE.

SERVES 6–8

INGREDIENTS

25ml/1½ tbsp dried juniper berries
10ml/2 tsp dried green peppercorns
5ml/1 tsp caster (superfine) sugar
45ml/3 tbsp vegetable oil, plus extra
  for greasing
30ml/2 tbsp lemon juice
2.25kg/5–5¼lb salmon, scaled,
  cleaned and boned for butterflying
salt
lemon wedges and fresh parsley
  sprigs, to garnish

1 Coarsely grind the juniper berries and peppercorns in a spice mill or in a mortar with a pestle. Put the ground spices in a small bowl and stir in the caster sugar, vegetable oil, lemon juice and salt to taste.

COOK'S TIP
It is worth keeping a jar of juniper berries in the spice rack, not merely so you can try this recipe, but also for using with game, or to give chicken or rabbit a gamey flavour. Juniper berries are also delicious with red cabbage.

2 Open the salmon like a book, skin side down. Spread the juniper mixture evenly over the flesh. Fold the salmon closed again and place it on a large plate. Cover and marinate in the refrigerator for at least 1 hour.

3 Preheat the grill (broiler). Open up the salmon again and place it, skin side down, on a large oiled baking sheet. Spoon any juniper mixture left on the plate over the fish.

4 Grill (broil) the salmon, keeping it about 10cm/4in from the heat, for 8–10 minutes or until the salmon is cooked and the flesh is opaque. Serve immediately, garnished with the lemon wedges and parsley.

SALMON IN A LEAF PARCEL

THIS IS AN INDIAN SPECIALITY FROM MUMBAI — OR, TO USE THE OLD NAME, BOMBAY. THERE IT
WOULD BE MADE USING SILVER POMFRET, BUT SALMON, WITH ITS ROBUST FLAVOUR, ALSO WORKS WELL.

SERVES 6

INGREDIENTS

50g/2oz fresh coconut, skinned and
finely grated, or 65g/2½oz/scant
1 cup desiccated (dry unsweetened
shredded) coconut, soaked in
30ml/2 tbsp water
1 large lemon, skin, pith and seeds
removed, roughly chopped
4 large garlic cloves, crushed
3 large fresh mild green chillies,
seeded and chopped
50g/2oz/1 cup fresh coriander
(cilantro), roughly chopped
25g/1oz/½ cup fresh mint leaves,
roughly chopped
5ml/1 tsp ground cumin
5ml/1 tsp sugar
2.5ml/½ tsp fenugreek seeds,
finely ground
5ml/1 tsp salt
2 large, whole banana leaves
6 salmon fillets, total weight about
1.2kg/2½lb, skinned

1 Place all the ingredients except the banana leaves and salmon in a food processor. Pulse to a fine paste. Scrape the mixture into a bowl, cover and chill for 30 minutes.

2 Make the parcels. Cut each banana leaf widthways into three and cut off the hard outside edge from each piece. Put the pieces of leaf and the edge strips in a bowl of hot water. Leave to soak for about 10 minutes.

3 Drain the leaf pieces and strips and gently wipe off any white residue. Rinse and pour over boiling water to soften. Drain again, then place the leaf pieces and strips, smooth side up, on a clean board to dry.

COOK'S TIP

Serve little rice parcels with the salmon. Fill six more banana leaf packages with cooked basmati rice, secure each one with a skewer and reheat on the grill.

4 Smear the top and bottom of each leaf with the coconut paste. Place one salmon fillet on each leaf. Bring the trimmed edge of the leaf over the salmon, then fold in the sides. Finally, bring up the remaining edge to cover the salmon and make a neat parcel. Tie each parcel securely with one of the soaked leaf strips.

5 Lay each parcel on a sheet of heavy-duty foil, bring up the edges and scrunch the tops together to seal. Position a lightly oiled grill rack over medium-hot coals to heat. Place the salmon parcels on the grill rack and cook for 10 minutes, turning over once.

6 Place the parcels on a board and leave to stand for 2–3 minutes – the salmon will continue to cook in the residual heat. Remove the foil, then transfer each banana leaf parcel to a plate, to be unwrapped at the table. Eat the fish straight out of the parcel.

SALMON WITH RED ONION MARMALADE

SALMON COOKS WELL ON THE BARBECUE BUT MAKE SURE IT IS AT LEAST 2.5 CM / 1 IN THICK TO MAKE IT EASY TO TURN THE PIECES ON THE GRILL. THE RED ONION MARMALADE IS RICH AND DELICIOUS.

SERVES 4

INGREDIENTS
    30ml/2 tbsp olive oil
    4 salmon fillets, 2.5cm/1in thick
    salt and ground black pepper

For the red onion marmalade
    50g/2oz/¼ cup butter
    5 medium red onions, thinly sliced
       and separated into rings
    175ml/6fl oz/¾ cup red wine vinegar
    50ml/2fl oz/¼ cup crème de cassis
    50ml/2fl oz/¼ cup grenadine
    50ml/2fl oz/¼ cup red wine

1 Brush the olive oil over the salmon fillets, working it into the flesh. Grind sea salt over the fish then repeat the process using black pepper. Set the salmon fillets aside.

2 Make the red onion marmalade. Melt the butter in a large, heavy pan and add the onion rings. Stir to coat them in butter, then sauté for 5–10 minutes, until the onions have softened.

3 Stir in the vinegar, crème de cassis, grenadine and wine and continue to cook the onions over a medium heat until the liquid has reduced. It should take about 10 minutes for the liquid to evaporate, leaving the onions covered with a rich glaze. Season well.

4 Brush the fish with a little more oil. Cook on a hot ridged griddle pan or in a hinged grill on the barbecue for 4–6 minutes on each side, or until cooked through. Serve immediately.

SALMON <u>WITH</u> SPICY PESTO

THIS IS A GREAT WAY TO BONE SALMON STEAKS TO GIVE A SOLID PIECE OF FISH. THE PESTO USES SUNFLOWER KERNELS AND CHILLI AS ITS FLAVOURING RATHER THAN THE CLASSIC BASIL AND PINE NUTS.

SERVES 4

INGREDIENTS
    4 salmon steaks, each about 225g/8oz
    30ml/2 tbsp sunflower oil
    finely grated rind and juice of 1 lime
    salt and ground black pepper

For the pesto
    6 fresh mild red chillies, seeded and
        roughly chopped
    2 garlic cloves
    30ml/2 tbsp pumpkin or
        sunflower seeds
    finely grated rind and juice of 1 lime
    75ml/5 tbsp olive oil

1 Place a salmon steak flat on a board. Insert a very sharp knife close to the top of the bone. Staying close to the bone all the time, cut to the end of the steak to release one side of the steak. Repeat with the other side.

2 Place one piece of salmon skin side down and hold it firmly with one hand. Insert a small sharp knife under the skin and, working away from you, cut the flesh off in a single piece. Repeat with the remaining salmon steaks.

3 Wrap each piece of fish into a circle, with the thinner end wrapped around the fatter end. Tie with string (twine). Place in a shallow bowl.

4 Rub the oil into the boneless fish rounds. Add the lime juice and rind to the bowl. Cover and marinate in the refrigerator for 2 hours.

5 Make the pesto. Put the chillies, garlic, pumpkin or sunflower seeds, lime rind and juice and seasoning into a food processor. Process until well mixed. With the machine running, gradually add the olive oil through the feeder tube. The pesto will slowly thicken and emulsify. Scrape it into a bowl. Preheat the grill (broiler).

6 Drain the salmon and place the rounds in a grill pan. Grill (broil) for 5 minutes on each side or until opaque. Serve with the spicy pesto.

COOK'S TIP
If any small bones remain in the salmon steaks after preparation, remove them with fish tweezers or a pair of new eyebrow tweezers kept for the purpose.

MEXICAN BARBECUE SALMON

THESE SALMON FILLETS COOK QUICKLY ON THE BARBECUE, AND BECAUSE THEY'VE BEEN MARINATED IN THE TOMATO SAUCE, THEY REMAIN BEAUTIFULLY MOIST AND SUCCULENT.

SERVES 4

INGREDIENTS

25g/1oz/2 tbsp butter
1 small red onion, finely chopped
1 garlic clove, crushed
6 plum tomatoes, diced
45ml/3 tbsp tomato ketchup
30ml/2 tbsp Dijon mustard
30ml/2 tbsp soft dark brown sugar
15ml/1 tbsp clear honey
5ml/1 tsp ground cayenne pepper
15ml/1 tbsp ancho chilli powder
15ml/1 tbsp paprika
15ml/1 tbsp Worcestershire sauce
4 salmon fillets, each about 175g/6oz
fresh flat leaf parsley sprigs,
  to garnish

3 Add the tomato ketchup, Dijon mustard, brown sugar, honey, cayenne pepper, chilli powder, paprika and Worcestershire sauce. Stir well, then simmer for a further 20 minutes. Pour the mixture into a food processor and process until smooth. Leave to cool.

4 Put the salmon fillets in a shallow dish, brush generously with the sauce and chill for at least 2 hours. Cook the salmon fillets on an oiled barbecue grill over medium-hot coals for 2–3 minutes on each side, brushing frequently with the sauce. Garnish and serve.

1 Melt the butter in a large, heavy pan and cook the onion and garlic gently for about 5 minutes until softened and translucent. Do not let the onion brown.

2 Add the diced plum tomatoes. Bring to the boil, then reduce the heat and simmer for 15 minutes. Stir the tomatoes occasionally with a wooden spoon so that they do not catch on the base of the pan.

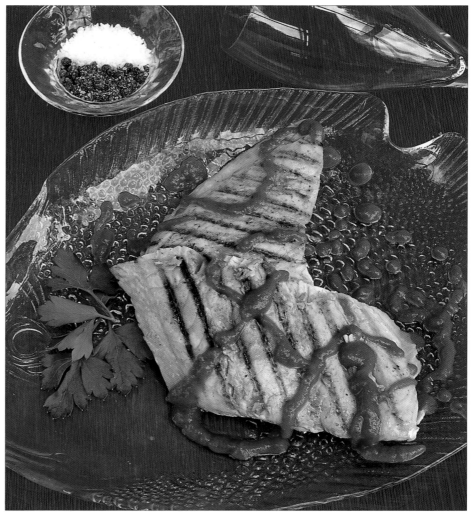

SALMON <u>WITH</u> TROPICAL FRUIT SALSA

FRESH SALMON, COOKED ON THE BARBECUE, IS GOOD ENOUGH TO SERVE ON ITS OWN, BUT TASTES EVEN BETTER WITH THIS COLOURFUL AND TASTY COMBINATION OF MANGO, PAPAYA AND CHILLI.

SERVES 4

INGREDIENTS

4 salmon steaks or fillets, each about
  175g/6oz
finely grated rind and juice
  of 1 lime
1 small, ripe mango
1 small, ripe papaya
1 fresh red chilli
45ml/3 tbsp chopped fresh
  coriander (cilantro)
salt and ground black pepper

COOK'S TIP
If fresh red chillies are not available, use about 2.5ml/½ tsp of chilli paste from a jar, or add a dash of chilli sauce.

1 Lay the pieces of salmon side by side in a wide dish and sprinkle over half the lime rind and juice. Season well.

2 Take a thick slice off either side of the mango stone (pit), and then remove the stone. Finely chop the mango flesh and put it in a bowl. Halve the papaya, scoop out and discard the seeds and remove the skin. Chop the flesh finely and add it to the mango.

3 Cut the chilli in half lengthways. For a milder flavour, remove the seeds, or leave the seeds in to make the salsa hot and spicy. Finely chop the chilli and add to the chopped fruit. Add the chopped fresh coriander to the bowl and mix gently with a large spoon.

4 Stir in the remaining lime rind and juice. Season to taste.

5 Cook the salmon on an oiled barbecue grill over medium-hot coals for 5–8 minutes, turning once. Serve with the tropical fruit salsa.

HOT SMOKED SALMON

*THIS IS A FANTASTIC WAY OF SMOKING SALMON ON A CHARCOAL
BARBECUE, USING SOAKED HICKORY WOOD CHIPS. MOJO, A SPICY
BUT NOT HOT SAUCE POPULAR IN CUBA, IS PERFECT TO CUT THE
RICHNESS OF THE HOT SMOKED SALMON.*

SERVES 6

INGREDIENTS
   6 salmon fillets, each about
      175g/6oz, with skin
   15ml/1 tbsp sunflower oil
   salt and ground black pepper
   2 handfuls hickory wood chips,
      soaked in cold water for at least
      30 minutes

For the mojo
   1 ripe mango, diced
   4 drained canned pineapple
      slices, diced
   1 small red onion, finely chopped
   1 fresh long mild red chilli, seeded
      and finely chopped
   15ml/1 tbsp good quality sweet
      chilli sauce
   grated rind and juice of 1 lime
   leaves from 1 small lemon basil plant
      or 45ml/3 tbsp fresh coriander
      (cilantro) leaves, chopped

1 Place the salmon fillets, skin-side
down, on a platter. Sprinkle the flesh
lightly with salt. Cover and leave in a
cool place for about 30 minutes.

2 Make the mojo by putting the mango,
diced pineapple, chopped onion and
seeded and chopped chilli in a bowl.

3 Add the chilli sauce, lime rind and
juice, and the herb leaves. Stir to mix
well. Cover tightly and leave in a cool
place until needed.

COOK'S TIP
Although canned pineapple slices give
a very satisfactory result, when sweet
pineapples are in season, you may
prefer to use fresh ones in the mojo.
You will need about half a medium-
sized pineapple. Slice off the skin,
remove the core and cut into chunks.

4 Pat the salmon fillets with kitchen
paper, then brush each one with a little
oil. Place the salmon fillets skin side
down on a lightly oiled grill rack over
medium-hot coals. Cover the barbecue
with a lid or tented heavy-duty foil and
cook the fish for about 3 minutes.

5 Drain the hickory chips into a
colander and sprinkle about a third of
them as evenly as possible over the
coals. Carefully drop them through the
slats in the grill racks, taking care not
to scatter the ash as you do so.

6 Replace the barbecue cover and
continue cooking for a further
8 minutes, adding a small handful
of hickory chips twice more during
this time. Serve the salmon hot or
cold, with the mojo.

TANGY GRILLED SALMON WITH PINEAPPLE

FRESH PINEAPPLE REALLY BRINGS OUT THE FLAVOUR OF SALMON. HERE, IT IS COMBINED WITH LIME JUICE TO MAKE A LIGHT AND REFRESHING DISH, WHICH TASTES GREAT WITH WILD RICE AND A SIMPLE GREEN SALAD TOSSED WITH A GRAPEFRUIT VINAIGRETTE DRESSING.

SERVES 4

INGREDIENTS
   grated rind and juice of 2 limes
   15ml/1 tbsp olive oil, plus extra
      for greasing
   1cm/½in piece fresh root ginger,
      peeled and grated
   1 garlic clove, crushed
   30ml/2 tbsp clear honey
   15ml/1 tbsp soy sauce
   4 salmon fillets, each about
      200g/7oz
   1 small pineapple
   30ml/2 tbsp sesame seeds
   ground black pepper
   fresh chives, to garnish
   wild rice and a green salad,
      to serve

COOK'S TIPS
• Watch the sesame seeds closely as
they brown very quickly.
• To cook wild rice, put it in a pan of
cold salted water. Bring to the boil,
then simmer for 30–40 minutes, or as
directed on the packet, until tender.
• Serve the grilled salmon with a
mixed leaf salad. For the dressing,
mix 45ml/3 tbsp grapefruit juice with
10ml/2 tsp balsamic vinegar and a
pinch each of salt, ground black
pepper and sugar, then whisk in
120ml/4fl oz/½ cup mild olive oil.

1 Make the marinade. Put the lime rind in a jug (pitcher) and stir in the lime juice, olive oil, ginger, garlic, honey and soy sauce. Taste and add a little ground black pepper. The inclusion of soy sauce in the marinade means that salt will probably not be needed.

2 Place the salmon fillets in a single layer in a shallow, non-metallic dish. Pour the marinade over the salmon. Cover and chill for at least 1 hour, turning the salmon halfway through.

3 Carefully cut the skin off the pineapple, removing as many of the small black "eyes" as possible. Cut the pineapple into four thick slices. Use an apple corer to remove the tough central core from each slice and cut away any remaining eyes with a small knife.

4 Preheat the grill (broiler) to high. Sprinkle the sesame seeds over a piece of foil and place under the grill for a minute or two until they turn golden brown. Set aside.

5 Grease the grill pan and cover with a layer of foil. Using a slotted spoon, remove the salmon fillets from the marinade and place them in a single layer on the foil. Add the pineapple rings, placing one on top of each piece of salmon.

6 Grill (broil) the fish and pineapple for 10 minutes, brushing occasionally with the marinade and turning everything over once, until the fish is cooked through and the pineapple rings are golden brown.

7 Transfer the fish to serving plates, placing each fillet on a bed of wild rice. Top with the pineapple slices. Sprinkle the sesame seeds over and garnish with the chives. Serve with a green salad.

PARTY FOODS

Time to show off now, as you transform salmon into impressive dinner party dishes.

Elegant doesn't have to mean elaborate, though, and many of these recipes are easy to prepare,

relying for their impact on the quality of the ingredients rather than complicated procedures.

The chapter opens with a selection of simple but stunning canapés, and moves on to main

attractions like Salmon Ceviche with Gin and Lime, and a Fish Terrine which will do

wonders for your reputation as a fine cook. For the buffet table, choose Whole Baked Salmon

and Smoked Salmon and Herb Roulade.

SMOKED SALMON PARCELS

NOTHING COULD BE SIMPLER THAN THESE PRETTY SALMON ROLLS. THERE ARE TWO DIFFERENT FILLINGS BUT BOTH ARE SO GOOD THAT THEY'RE LIKELY TO DISAPPEAR AT THE SAME SPEED.

MAKES ABOUT 20

INGREDIENTS
   350g/12oz best quality
     smoked salmon
   2 lemons, cut in quarters and a
     bunch of fresh dill, to garnish

For the fish filling
   225g/8oz smoked mackerel
     fillet, skinned
   45ml/3 tbsp crème fraîche
   ground black pepper

For the cheese and herb filling
   bunch of fresh mixed herbs, such
     as chives, parsley and chervil
   225g/8oz/1 cup ricotta cheese
   salt and ground black pepper

1 For the fish filling, chop the mackerel roughly and place in a bowl. Mash with the crème fraîche. Season with pepper.

2 Make the cheese filling. Chop the herbs finely and stir them into the ricotta cheese in a bowl. Season with plenty of salt and pepper.

3 Cut the smoked salmon into strips, about 2.5 x 7.5cm/1 x 3in. Put a teaspoon of the fish filling at one end of a strip and roll up neatly. Continue until half the salmon has been used, then repeat the procedure with the cheese filling. Arrange the rolls on a platter and garnish with the lemon and dill.

SALMON TRIANGLES

THESE ELEGANT PARTY PIECES TAKE A LITTLE TIME TO MAKE, BUT THEY CAN BE PREPARED IN ADVANCE WITH THE FINAL TOUCHES ADDED JUST BEFORE YOUR GUESTS ARRIVE.

MAKES 12

INGREDIENTS
   2 eggs
   3–4 slices dark rye bread
   115g/4oz poached salmon
   coriander (cilantro) leaves, to garnish

For the lime and coriander mayonnaise
   45–60ml/3–4 tbsp mayonnaise
   5ml/1 tsp chopped fresh coriander
    (cilantro)
   5ml/1 tsp freshly squeezed
    lime juice
   salt and ground black pepper

1 Bring a pan of water to the boil. Reduce the heat, then add the eggs. Cook for 12 minutes, then plunge the eggs into cold water to arrest further cooking. When cold, shell the hard-boiled eggs and slice them.

2 Cut the rye bread into 12 triangular pieces, using a sharp knife.

3 Make the lime and coriander mayonnaise. Combine the mayonnaise, chopped coriander and lime juice, and season to taste.

4 Top each bread triangle with a slice of egg, a small portion of salmon and a teaspoon of mayonnaise. Garnish with a coriander leaf. Chill until ready to serve.

COOK'S TIP
Using this recipe as a guide, many different canapés can be made. Try substituting cherry tomato slices for the egg and topping the salmon with a mixture of mayonnaise and red pesto, or use sliced cucumber and top the salmon with lemon-flavoured mayonnaise. For a luxury note, use a neutral mayonnaise and add a spoonful of caviar. The black roe looks very dramatic with the pale pink salmon.

SALMON AND TROUT CANAPÉS

THESE TINY LITTLE BITES ARE IDEAL FOR SERVING WITH A GLASS OF CHILLED SPARKLING WINE OR AS PART OF A FINGER BUFFET.

<u>MAKES 44</u>

For the salmon and dill squares
  15ml/1 tbsp olive oil
  175g/6oz salmon fillet, skinned
  500g/1¼lb sliced pumpernickel
    bread
  mayonnaise, for spreading
  1 small cucumber, thinly sliced
  60ml/4 tbsp sour cream
  30ml/2 tbsp chopped fresh dill
  10ml/2 tsp lemon juice
  ½ red (bell) pepper, seeded and
    finely chopped
  salt and ground black pepper

For the smoked trout squares
  5 thin slices white bread, toasted
  75g/3oz/scant ½ cup cream cheese
    with garlic and herbs
  75g/3oz smoked trout, skinned
  finely grated rind of 2 lemons
  lemon wedges, to garnish

1 Heat the oil in a griddle pan. Season the salmon fillet well on both sides and fry for 5–8 minutes or until the flesh is opaque. Remove from the pan and leave to cool.

2 Using a fluted 5cm/2in cutter, cut out 24 squares from the sliced pumpernickel. Spread a little mayonnaise on each bread square and top with a cucumber slice.

3 Flake the salmon into bitesize pieces and remove any remaining bones. Put the fish in a bowl and mix with the sour cream, dill and lemon juice. Season with salt and pepper to taste.

4 Spread a little of the mixture on each pumpernickel square and top with pieces of red pepper.

5 Make the smoked trout squares. Trim the crusts from the toast and spread a fifth of the cheese on each slice. Cut each slice into four squares.

6 Cut the smoked trout into pieces and divide among the toast squares.

7 Sprinkle the lemon rind over the trout and season with plenty of black pepper.

8 Arrange the canapés on a large serving platter or separate plates and garnish with the lemon wedges. Chill until ready to serve.

SMOKED SALMON PANCAKES WITH PINE NUTS

THESE SIMPLE PANCAKES TAKE ONLY MINUTES TO PREPARE AND ARE PERFECT FOR A SPECIAL OCCASION. SMOKED SALMON IS DELICIOUS WITH FRESH BASIL AND COMBINES WELL WITH TOASTED PINE NUTS AND A SPOONFUL OF CRÈME FRAÎCHE OR SOUR CREAM.

MAKES 12–16

INGREDIENTS
   120ml/4fl oz/½ cup milk
   115g/4oz/1 cup self-raising
    (self-rising) flour
   1 egg
   30ml/2 tbsp pesto
   vegetable oil, for frying
   200ml/7fl oz/scant 1 cup crème
    fraîche or sour cream
   75g/3oz smoked salmon
   15ml/1 tbsp pine nuts, toasted
   salt and ground black pepper
   12–16 fresh basil sprigs, to garnish

COOK'S TIP
If not serving immediately, cover the pancakes with a dishtowel and keep warm in an oven preheated to 140°C/275°F/Gas 1.

1 Pour half the milk into a mixing bowl. Add the flour, egg and pesto and mix to a smooth batter.

2 Add the remainder of the milk and mix until evenly blended. Season the batter with salt and pepper.

3 Heat the vegetable oil in a large frying pan. Spoon the batter into the heated oil in small heaps. Allow about 30 seconds for the pancakes to cook, then turn and cook briefly on the other side. Continue cooking pancakes until all the batter has been used.

4 Arrange the pancakes on a serving plate and top each one with a spoonful of crème fraîche or sour cream.

5 Cut the salmon into pieces to fit the top of the pancakes and lightly place them on top of the cream.

6 Sprinkle each pancake with pine nuts and garnish with the fresh basil. Serve immediately.

SMOKED SALMON PIZZETTES

FOR A SOPHISTICATED MEAL, DISPENSE WITH THE APPETIZER AND SERVE THESE PIZZAS WITH PRE-MEAL DRINKS. BLACK LUMPFISH ROE MAKES A DRAMATIC CONTRAST TO THE COLOUR OF THE SALMON.

MAKES 10–12

INGREDIENTS
    15ml/1 tbsp olive oil
    75–115g/3–4oz smoked salmon,
      cut into strips
    60ml/4 tbsp crème fraîche or
      sour cream
    30ml/2 tbsp black lumpfish roe
    chives, to garnish

For the dough
    175g/6oz/1½ cups strong white
      (bread) flour
    1.5ml/¼ tsp salt
    5ml/1 tsp easy-blend (rapid-rise)
      dried yeast
    120–150ml/4–5fl oz/½–⅔ cup
      lukewarm water
    15ml/1 tbsp olive oil
    15ml/1 tbsp chopped fresh chives

1 Make the dough. Sift the flour and salt into a mixing bowl, stir in the yeast, then make a well in the centre and add the liquids. Mix with a spoon to a soft dough.

2 Knead the dough until smooth and elastic, then place in a bowl, cover with clear film (plastic wrap) and leave in a warm place for about 1 hour or until the dough has doubled in bulk.

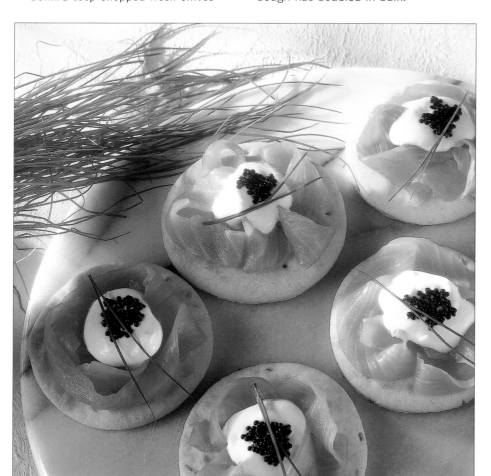

3 Preheat the oven to 200°C/400°F/ Gas 6. Knock back (punch down) the dough and knead it gently, adding the chives until evenly mixed.

4 Roll out the dough on a lightly floured surface to about 3mm/⅛in thick. Using a 7.5cm/3in plain round cutter, stamp out 10–12 circles.

5 Place the bases well apart on two greased baking sheets, prick all over with a fork, then brush with the oil. Bake for 10–15 minutes until crisp.

6 Arrange the smoked salmon on top, then spoon on the crème fraîche or sour cream. Top with lumpfish roe and garnish with chives. Serve immediately.

POTATO BLINIS WITH SMOKED SALMON

THESE CRISP, LIGHT PANCAKES ORIGINATED IN RUSSIA, WHERE THEY ARE SERVED WITH THE FINEST CAVIAR, BUT THEY ARE ALSO GOOD WITH SALMON ROE.

SERVES 6 AS PART OF A BUFFET

INGREDIENTS
   1 potato, about 115g/4oz, boiled
     and mashed
   15ml/1 tbsp easy-blend (rapid-rise)
     dried yeast
   175g/6oz/1½ cups plain
     (all-purpose) flour
   300ml/½ pint/1¼ cups
     lukewarm water
   oil, for greasing
   90ml/6 tbsp sour cream
   6 slices smoked salmon
   salt and ground black pepper
   lemon slices, to garnish

1 Mix the potato, yeast, flour, salt and pepper with the water to make a smooth dough. Cover with clear film (plastic wrap) and leave to rise in a warm place for 30 minutes until doubled in bulk.

2 Heat a non-stick frying pan and add a little oil. Drop spoonfuls of the mixture on to the pan.

3 Cook the blinis for 2 minutes until lightly golden on the underside. Toss with a spatula and cook on the second side. Remove each batch as it cooks and keep warm.

4 To serve, top each blini with a little sour cream and a small folded slice of smoked salmon. Garnish with black pepper and a small slice of lemon.

VARIATION
For an alternative topping, mix 200g/7oz/ scant 1 cup cream cheese with 15ml/ 1 tbsp chopped parsley or dill. Spread on the blinis and top with the salmon. Add slivers of sweet pickled cherry chillies or a spoonful of salmon roe.

SALMON AND RICE TRIANGLES

IN JAPAN, WHERE THESE ORIGINATED, THEY ARE OFTEN USED FOR PACKED LUNCHES OR PICNICS, BUT WOULD ALSO MAKE ELEGANT PARTY PIECES. THEY ARE GREAT FUN TO MAKE AND LOOK MARVELLOUS.

SERVES 4 AS PART OF A BUFFET

INGREDIENTS

- 1 salmon steak
- 15ml/1 tbsp salt
- 450g/1lb/4 cups freshly cooked Japanese short grain rice
- 4 umeboshi (plum pickles)
- ½ sheet yaki-nori seaweed, cut into four equal strips
- white and black sesame seeds, for sprinkling

1 Grill (broil) the salmon steak for 4–5 minutes on each side, until the flesh flakes easily when it is tested with the tip of a sharp knife. Set aside to cool.

2 Put the salt in a bowl. Spoon a quarter of the warm cooked rice into a small rice bowl.

3 Make a hole in the middle of the rice and put in one umeboshi. Smooth the rice carefully over to cover it completely.

4 Wet the palms of both hands with cold water, then rub the salt evenly on to your palms.

5 Empty the rice and umeboshi from the bowl on to one hand. Use both hands to shape the rice into a triangular shape, using firm but not heavy pressure. Make three more rice triangles in the same way.

6 Flake the salmon, discarding any skin and any bones. Mix the flaked salmon into the remaining rice, then shape it into triangles as before.

7 Wrap a strip of yaki-nori around each of the umeboshi triangles. Sprinkle sesame seeds on the salmon triangles. Serve immediately or cool completely, then wrap each in foil or clear film (plastic wrap).

COOK'S TIP
Always use warm rice to make triangles as it is easier to mould.

SALMON MARINATED WITH THAI SPICES

MARINATING THE FISH IN AN AROMATIC MIXTURE OF GINGER, LEMON GRASS, LIME LEAVES, CHILLIES AND SALT NOT ONLY CURES IT, BUT ALSO IMBUES THE SALMON WITH DELECTABLE FLAVOURS.

SERVES 4–6 AS PART OF A BUFFET

INGREDIENTS
  tail piece of 1 salmon, about
    675g/1½lb, halved and boned
    to produce two fillets
  20ml/4 tsp coarse sea salt
  20ml/4 tsp sugar
  2.5cm/1in piece fresh root
    ginger, grated
  2 lemon grass stalks, coarse outer
    leaves removed, thinly sliced
  4 kaffir lime leaves, finely chopped
    or shredded
  grated rind of 1 lime
  1 fresh red chilli, seeded and
    finely chopped
  5ml/1 tsp black peppercorns,
    coarsely crushed
  30ml/2 tbsp chopped fresh
    coriander (cilantro)
  fresh coriander (cilantro) and kaffir
    limes, to garnish

For the dressing
  150ml/¼ pint/⅔ cup mayonnaise
  juice of ½ lime
  10ml/2 tsp chopped fresh
    coriander (cilantro)

1 Remove any remaining bones from the salmon, using a pair of tweezers. In a bowl, mix together the salt, sugar, ginger, lemon grass, lime leaves, lime rind, chilli, peppercorns and chopped fresh coriander.

2 Place one-quarter of the spice mixture in a shallow non-metallic dish. Place one salmon fillet, skin side down, on top of the spices. Spread two-thirds of the remaining mixture over the flesh then place the remaining fillet on top, flesh side down. Sprinkle the rest of the spice mixture over the fish.

3 Cover the fish with foil, then place a board on top. Add some weights, such as clean cans of fruit. Chill for 4–5 days, turning the fish daily in the spicy brine that collects in the base of the dish.

4 Make the dressing by mixing the mayonnaise, lime juice and chopped coriander in a bowl.

5 Scrape the spices off the fish. Slice it as thinly as possible. Serve with the lime dressing, garnished with coriander and wedges of kaffir limes.

FISH TERRINE

THIS COLOURFUL LAYERED TERRINE MAKES A SPECTACULAR PRESENTATION FOR A SPECIAL OCCASION.
IT IS PERFECT FOR ENTERTAINING SINCE IT IS BEST MADE THE DAY BEFORE AND CHILLED OVERNIGHT.

SERVES 6 AS PART OF A BUFFET

INGREDIENTS
450g/1lb white fish fillets, skinned
225–275g/8–10oz thinly sliced
    smoked salmon
2 egg whites, chilled
1.5ml/¼ tsp each salt and
    white pepper
pinch of freshly grated nutmeg
250ml/8fl oz/1 cup whipping cream
60g/2oz baby spinach leaves
lemon mayonnaise, to serve

1 Cut the white fish fillets into 2.5cm/1in pieces, removing any bones as you work. Spread out the fish pieces on a plate and cover with clear film (plastic wrap). Place in the freezer for about 15 minutes until very cold.

2 Lightly grease a 1.2 litre/2 pint/5 cup terrine or loaf pan. Line the base with baking parchment, then line the base and sides of the pan with smoked salmon slices, letting them hang over the edge. Preheat the oven to 180°C/350°F/Gas 4.

3 Put the pieces of chilled fish in a food processor and whizz to a very smooth purée, stopping the machine several times to scrape down the sides.

4 Add the egg whites, one at a time, then the salt, pepper and nutmeg. With the machine running, pour in the cream through the feeder tube. Stop as soon as it is blended. (If overprocessed, the cream will thicken too much.)

5 Transfer the fish mixture to a large glass bowl. Put the spinach leaves into the food processor and process to a purée. Add one-third of the fish mixture to the spinach and process until just combined, scraping down the sides once or twice.

6 Spread half the plain fish mixture in the base of the pan and smooth it level. Spoon the green fish mixture over the top and smooth the surface, then cover with the remaining plain mixture and smooth the top.

7 Fold the overhanging pieces of salmon over the top to enclose the mixture. Tap the pan to settle the mixture and remove any air pockets, then cover the terrine with a double layer of foil.

8 Put the terrine in a roasting pan and pour in enough boiling water to come halfway up the sides of the terrine. Bake for about 1 hour, until a skewer inserted in the centre comes out clean. Allow to cool, wrap well and chill for 3–4 hours or overnight, until firm.

9 To serve the terrine, invert on a board and slice. Arrange slices on individual plates and serve with lemon mayonnaise.

SALMON CEVICHE <u>WITH</u> GIN <u>AND</u> LIME

MARINATING RAW SALMON IN A MIXTURE OF GIN AND LIME JUICE CHANGES THE TEXTURE OF THE FISH, EFFECTIVELY "COOKING" IT. THE FLAVOUR IS SUPERB.

<u>SERVES 4 AS PART OF A BUFFET</u>

INGREDIENTS
    675g/1½lb salmon fillet, skinned
    1 small red onion, thinly sliced
    6 chives
    6 fennel sprigs
    3 fresh parsley sprigs
    2 limes
    30ml/2 tbsp gin
    45ml/3 tbsp olive oil
    sea salt and ground black pepper
    salad leaves, to serve

1 Cut the salmon fillet into thin slices, removing any remaining bones with tweezers. Lay the pieces in a wide, shallow non-metallic dish.

2 Sprinkle over the onion slices and strew with the chives, fennel and parsley sprigs. Using a canelle knife, remove a few fine strips of rind from the limes and reserve for the garnish. Cut off the remaining rind, avoiding the pith, and slice it roughly.

COOK'S TIP
• When preparing salmon in this way, it is vital to use very fresh fish from a reputable source. Tell the fishmonger you intend making ceviche, explaining that the fish will not be cooked in the conventional way, but that the texture will be altered by marinating it in lime juice, gin and olive oil.
• Serve the ceviche on the day you prepare it. It needs to be chilled for 4 hours, but do not leave it for much longer before serving.

3 Squeeze the lime juice into a jug (pitcher). Add the roughly sliced rind, with the gin and olive oil. Stir in sea salt and black pepper to taste. Pour the mixture over the fish and stir gently to coat each piece thoroughly.

4 Cover the dish and chill for 4 hours, stirring occasionally. To serve, arrange the slices of marinated fish on a platter, with the salad leaves. Sprinkle over the reserved strips of lime rind.

SMOKED SALMON AND HERB ROULADE

MAKE THE MOST OF A SMALL AMOUNT OF SMOKED SALMON BY USING IT IN THE FILLING FOR THIS DELICATELY FLAVOURED ROULADE. MAKE THE ROULADE IN ADVANCE TO GIVE IT TIME TO COOL, BUT DON'T PUT IT IN THE REFRIGERATOR OR IT WILL LOSE ITS LIGHT TEXTURE.

SERVES 6–8 AS PART OF A BUFFET

INGREDIENTS
  25g/1oz/2 tbsp butter
  25g/1oz/¼ cup plain
    (all-purpose) flour
  175ml/6fl oz/¾ cup milk, warm
  3 large eggs, separated
  50g/2oz/⅔ cup freshly grated
    Parmesan cheese
  60ml/4 tbsp chopped fresh dill
  30ml/2 tbsp chopped fresh parsley
  150ml/¼ pint/⅔ cup full fat crème
    fraîche or sour cream
  115g/4oz smoked salmon
  salt and ground black pepper
  lamb's lettuce, to garnish

1 Melt the butter in a heavy pan, stir in the flour and cook over a low heat to a thick paste. Gradually add the milk, whisking constantly until the sauce boils and thickens, then cook for 1–2 minutes more. Stir in the egg yolks, two-thirds of the Parmesan cheese, the parsley and half the dill. Add salt and ground black pepper to taste.

2 Prepare a 33 x 28cm/13 x 11in Swiss roll tin (jelly roll pan) and preheat the oven to 180°C/350°F/Gas 4. Whisk the egg whites and fold into the yolk mixture, then pour into the tin or pan and bake for 12–15 minutes. Cover with baking parchment and set aside for 10–15 minutes, then tip out on to another sheet of parchment, this time sprinkled with a little Parmesan. Leave to cool.

3 Coarsely chop the smoked salmon, then mix it in a bowl with the crème fraîche or sour cream and remaining chopped dill. Stir gently but thoroughly, then taste and add salt and pepper as needed.

4 Peel off the lining paper from the roulade, spread the filling evenly over the surface and roll up, then leave to firm up in a cold place. Sprinkle with the rest of the Parmesan and garnish with the lamb's lettuce.

WHOLE BAKED SALMON

FARMED SALMON HAS MADE THIS FISH MORE AFFORDABLE AND LESS OF A LUXURY BUT A WHOLE SALMON STILL FEATURES AS A CENTREPIECE AT PARTIES. TRADITIONALLY IT IS ACCOMPANIED BY VARIOUS SALADS AND A BOWL OF MAYONNAISE.

SERVES 10 AS PART OF A BUFFET

INGREDIENTS
2.25–2.75kg/5–6lb fresh whole
    salmon, cleaned and scaled
30ml/2 tbsp oil
1 lemon
salt and ground black pepper
lemon wedges, pared cucumber
    ribbons and fresh dill sprigs,
    to garnish

1 Preheat the oven to 150°C/300°F/ Gas 2. Note the weight of the salmon then wash it and dry it well, inside and out. Pour half the oil on to a large piece of strong foil and place the fish in the centre.

2 Put a few slices of lemon inside the salmon and arrange some more on the top. Season well and sprinkle over the remaining oil. Wrap up the foil to make a loose parcel.

COOK'S TIPS
• Use wild salmon if you can afford it, or buy from a farm where the salmon are humanely treated.
• Use extra wide, extra long foil – sometimes described as turkey foil – to wrap the salmon.
• To make the cucumber ribbons, square off but do not peel a cucumber, then draw a potato peeler down its length.

3 Put the parcel on another sheet of foil or a baking sheet and transfer to the oven. Bake for 8 minutes per 450g/1lb. Check the fish towards the end of cooking and remove from the oven when the flesh is opaque right through. Leave to cool in the foil for 15 minutes.

4 Remove the foil, draining any juices into a jug (pitcher). Use in any recipe requiring fish stock. Peel off the salmon skin. When it is cold, slide the salmon on to a large platter and garnish with lemon wedges, cucumber pared into thin ribbons and sprigs of dill.

SALMON WITH RICE IN PUFF PASTRY

THIS VARIATION ON THE FAMOUS KOULIBIAK MAKES A DRAMATIC PARTY DISH. LIKE THE ORIGINAL, IT ENCASES SALMON, RICE AND HARD-BOILED EGGS IN PASTRY.

SERVES 6 AS PART OF A BUFFET

INGREDIENTS
    450g/1lb puff pastry, thawed
        if frozen
    1 egg, beaten
    3 hard-boiled eggs
    90ml/6 tbsp single (light) cream
    200g/7oz/1¾ cups cooked long
        grain rice
    30ml/2 tbsp finely chopped fresh
        parsley
    10ml/2 tsp chopped fresh tarragon
    675g/1½lb fresh salmon fillets
    40g/1½oz/3 tbsp butter
    juice of ½ lemon
    salt and ground black pepper

1 Preheat the oven to 190°C/375°F/ Gas 5. Roll out two-thirds of the pastry into a large oval, measuring about 35cm/14in in length. Cut into a curved fish shape and place on a baking sheet. Cut narrow strips from the trimmings.

2 Brush one side of each strip with a little of the beaten egg and secure in place around the rim of the pastry to make a raised edge. Prick the base all over with a fork, then bake for 8–10 minutes until the sides have risen well and the pastry is lightly golden. Leave to cool.

COOK'S TIP
If the pastry seems to be browning too quickly, cover it with foil during cooking and remove from the oven for the last 5 minutes. It is important that the "fish" cooks for the recommended time, so that the salmon is cooked through.

3 In a bowl, mash the hard-boiled eggs with the cream, then stir in the cooked rice. Add the parsley and tarragon and season well. Spoon this mixture on to the prepared pastry.

4 Cut the salmon into 2cm/¾in chunks. Melt the butter until it starts to sizzle, then add the salmon. Turn the pieces over in the butter so that they begin to colour but do not cook through.

5 Remove from the heat and arrange the salmon pieces on top of the rice, piled in the centre. Stir the lemon juice into the butter in the pan, then spoon the mixture over the salmon pieces.

6 Roll out the remaining pastry and cut out a semi-circular piece to cover the head portion and a tail shape to cover the tail. Brush both pieces of pastry with a little beaten egg and place on top of the fish, pressing down firmly to secure. Score a criss-cross pattern on the tail.

7 Cut the remaining pastry into small circles and, starting from the tail end, arrange the circles in overlapping lines to represent scales. Add an extra one for an eye. Brush the whole fish shape with the remaining beaten egg.

8 Bake for 10 minutes, then reduce the temperature to 160°C/325°F/Gas 3 and cook for a further 15–20 minutes until the pastry is evenly golden. Slide the fish on to a serving plate and serve.

VARIATION
If time is short you may prefer to use this simplified version of the recipe. Roll two-thirds of the pastry into a rectangle, then make pastry edges to contain the filling. Part bake the pastry shape, then add the filling. Top with plain, rolled out pastry and bake as above.

SAUCES

The perfect sauce neither makes nor mars a dish but simply supports the main ingredients in such a way that it would be inconceivable to serve one without the other. Sorrel Sauce is a good example of this. Its tangy flavour and creamy consistency make it the perfect companion for grilled or fried salmon steaks, while Watercress Cream is a winner with either salmon or trout.

YOGURT AND MINT SAUCE

THIS LIGHT AND DELICATE SAUCE IS A PERFECT BALANCE FOR THE RICHNESS OF SALMON. IT WOULD ALSO BE VERY GOOD WITH EITHER FRESH OR SMOKED TROUT. A MIXED GREEN LEAF AND HERB SALAD MAKES A PERFECT ACCOMPANIMENT.

MAKES ABOUT 150ML/¼ PINT/⅔ CUP

INGREDIENTS
    ½ large cucumber
    6 fresh mint leaves
    150ml/¼ pint/⅔ cup natural Greek
      (US strained plain) yogurt
    salt and ground black pepper

COOK'S TIP
This sauce is delicious with smoked salmon or griddled fresh salmon in a pitta pocket. Toast pitta breads briefly, split in half widthways, then open out each pocket and fill with salmon, salad leaves and the yogurt and mint sauce.

1 Peel the cucumber, slice it in half lengthways and scoop out the seeds with a teaspoon.

2 Chop the mint leaves and put them in a bowl. Grate the cucumber into a sieve, salt lightly and drain for about 30 minutes.

3 Add the yogurt to the chopped mint leaves and mix well. Squeeze out any excess juice from the cucumber, then stir it into the bowl with the yogurt and mint. Season with black pepper to taste. Cover and chill until ready to serve.

SORREL SAUCE

THE SHARP, ALMOST LEMONY FLAVOUR OF THE SORREL SAUCE MAKES IT IDEAL FOR SERVING WITH SALMON OR TROUT. YOUNG SORREL LEAVES HAVE THE BEST FLAVOUR, BUT CAN BE DIFFICULT TO OBTAIN, SO IT IS WORTH GROWING THE HERB IN A POT OR KITCHEN GARDEN.

MAKES ABOUT 120ML/4FL OZ/½ CUP

INGREDIENTS

25g/1oz/2 tbsp butter
4 shallots, finely chopped
90ml/6 tbsp crème fraîche or double (heavy) cream
100g/3½oz fresh sorrel leaves, washed and patted dry
salt and ground black pepper

1 Melt the butter in a heavy pan over a medium heat.

2 Add the shallots and fry for 2–3 minutes, stirring frequently, until just softened.

3 Stir in the crème fraîche or double (heavy) cream. Add the sorrel leaves to the shallots and cook until the sorrel is completely wilted, stirring constantly.

4 Spoon the cream and sorrel mixture into a food processor and process for just long enough to chop the sorrel and distribute the pieces evenly throughout the sauce.

5 Return the sauce to the clean pan, season with salt and pepper and heat gently. Serve hot.

VARIATION
If sorrel is not available, use finely chopped watercress instead.

BUTTER SAUCE

*THE LEMONY BUTTER SAUCE IS A QUICK AND EASY ACCOMPANIMENT TO VIRTUALLY ANY FISH BUT IS
ESPECIALLY GOOD WITH SALMON OR FILLETS OF TROUT.*

MAKES ABOUT 120ML/4FL OZ/½ CUP

INGREDIENTS
 75g/3oz/6 tbsp butter
 grated rind and juice of ½ lemon
 15–30ml/1–2 tbsp cold water

VARIATION
If you like, use a lime instead of the half
lemon for a change of flavour.

1 Melt the butter, then whisk in the
lemon rind, lemon juice and cold water.

2 Season the sauce with salt and
ground black pepper to taste. Simmer
for 2–3 minutes and serve.

COOK'S TIP
It is important not to let the butter
get too hot when making the sauce.
If it darkens, it will not only spoil the
appearance of the sauce, but will also
ruin the delicate flavour.

SUMMER HERB MARINADE

*RAID THE HERB GARDEN AND MAKE THIS FRESH-TASTING MARINADE. IT IS GREAT FOR SALMON OR
TROUT, BUT ALSO WORKS WELL WITH CHICKEN, PORK OR LAMB.*

MAKES ABOUT 150ML/¼ PINT/⅔ CUP

INGREDIENTS
 large handful of fresh herb sprigs,
  such as chervil, thyme, parsley,
  sage, chives, rosemary or oregano
 45ml/3 tbsp tarragon vinegar
 1 garlic clove, crushed
 2 spring onions (scallions), chopped
 90ml/6 tbsp olive oil
 salt and ground black pepper

1 Remove and discard any coarse stalks
or damaged leaves from the herbs, then
chop them very finely.

3 Use as a marinade for salmon, pork,
chicken, or lamb. Spread the fish or
meat in a single layer in a dish. Pour
over the marinade and mix. Marinate
fish for 2–3 hours; meat for 4–6 hours.

2 Mix the vinegar, garlic and spring
onions in a bowl. Whisk in the olive oil,
then add the chopped herbs and mix
well. Season with salt and pepper.

4 Use the marinade to baste the fish or
meat occasionally during cooking.

COOK'S TIP
Use a sharp cook's knife or a mezzaluna
to chop the herbs. It is best to avoid
using a food processor. Unless you
are very careful, the blade of a food
processor will rapidly reduce the herbs
to a soggy mess by releasing their
natural moisture. This not only looks
unattractive, but also muddies the
flavour of the marinade.

WATERCRESS CREAM

THE DELICATE GREEN COLOUR OF THIS CREAM SAUCE LOOKS WONDERFUL AGAINST PINK-FLESHED FISH SUCH AS SALMON OR SEA TROUT. THE FLAVOUR IS COMPLEMENTARY, TOO.

MAKES ABOUT 250ML/8FL OZ/1 CUP

INGREDIENTS
    2 bunches watercress or
      rocket (arugula)
    25g/1oz/2 tbsp butter
    2 shallots, chopped
    25g/1oz/¼ cup plain
      (all-purpose) flour
    150ml/¼ pint/⅔ cup hot
      fish stock
    150ml/¼ pint/⅔ cup dry
      white wine
    5ml/1 tsp anchovy essence
      (extract)
    150ml/¼ pint/⅔ cup single
      (light) cream
    lemon juice
    salt and cayenne pepper

3 Remove the pan from the heat and gradually stir in the fish stock and wine. Return the pan to the heat and bring the sauce to the boil, stirring constantly. Reduce the heat and simmer gently for 2–3 minutes, stirring occasionally.

4 Strain the sauce into a clean pan, then stir in the watercress or rocket, with the anchovy essence and cream. Warm over a low heat. Season with salt and cayenne pepper and sharpen with lemon juice to taste. Serve immediately.

1 Trim the watercress or rocket of any bruised leaves and coarse stalks. Blanch in boiling water for 5 minutes. Drain, refresh under cold running water, and drain again in a sieve or colander. Press the watercress or rocket against the sides of the sieve or colander with a spoon to remove excess moisture. Chop finely and set aside.

2 Melt the butter in a pan and fry the shallots over a medium heat for 3–4 minutes, until soft. Stir in the flour and cook for 1–2 minutes.

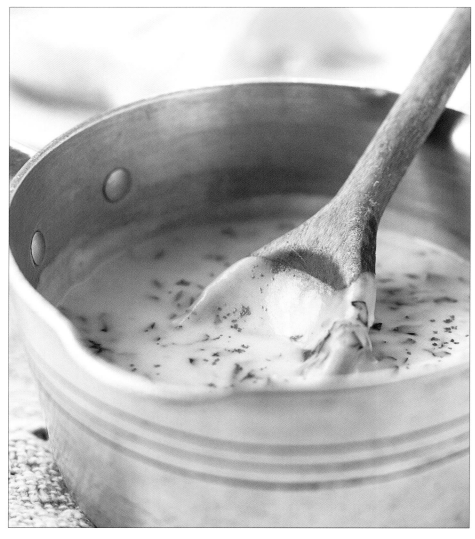

NEVER-FAIL MAYONNAISE

SOME PEOPLE FIND CLASSIC MAYONNAISE DIFFICULT TO MAKE, BUT THIS VERSION COULDN'T BE EASIER. THE ESSENTIAL THING IS TO HAVE ALL THE INGREDIENTS AT ROOM TEMPERATURE.

MAKES ABOUT 350ML/12FL OZ/1½ CUPS

INGREDIENTS

   1 egg, plus 1 egg yolk
   5ml/1 tsp Dijon mustard
   juice of 1 large lemon
   175ml/6fl oz/¾ cup olive oil
   175ml/6fl oz/¾ cup grapeseed,
     sunflower or corn oil
   salt and ground white pepper

COOK'S TIPS
• Be aware that this recipe contains raw eggs. If this is a concern, use bought mayonnaise instead.
• To make the mayonnaise even more glossy, beat in about 15ml/1 tbsp boiling water at the end, if you like.

1 Put the whole egg and yolk in a food processor and process for 20 seconds. Add the mustard, half the lemon juice and a generous pinch of salt and pepper. Put on the lid, then process the mixture for about 30 seconds more, until thoroughly mixed.

2 With the motor running, pour in the oils through the feeder tube in a thin, steady stream. When both oils have been incorporated and the mayonnaise is pale and thick, taste and add more lemon juice and seasoning if necessary. Scrape the mayonnaise into a bowl.

BEURRE BLANC

LEGEND HAS IT THAT THIS EXQUISITE SAUCE WAS INVENTED BY A COOK WHO FORGOT TO PUT EGG YOLKS INTO A BÉARNAISE SAUCE. WHETHER OR NOT THIS IS TRUE DOESN'T MATTER: THIS LIGHT SAUCE GOES PERFECTLY WITH POACHED OR GRILLED SALMON OR TROUT.

MAKES ABOUT 150ML/¼ PINT/⅔ CUP

INGREDIENTS
    3 shallots, very finely chopped
    45ml/3 tbsp dry white wine or
      court-bouillon
    45ml/3 tbsp white wine vinegar or
      tarragon vinegar
    115g/4oz/½ cup chilled unsalted
      (sweet) butter, diced
    lemon juice (optional)
    salt and ground white pepper

1 Put the shallots in a small pan with the wine or court-bouillon and vinegar. Bring to the boil and cook over a high heat until only about 30ml/2 tbsp liquid remains in the pan.

2 Remove the pan from the heat and leave to cool until the reduced liquid is just lukewarm.

3 Whisk in the chilled butter, one piece at a time, to make a pale, creamy sauce. Taste the sauce, then season with salt and pepper and add a little lemon juice to taste if you like.

4 If you are not serving the sauce immediately, keep it warm in the top of a double boiler set over barely simmering water.

HOLLANDAISE SAUCE

THIS RICH SAUCE GOES WELL WITH ANY POACHED FISH. SERVE IT WARM. AS THE EGG YOLKS ARE BARELY COOKED, IT IS NOT A GOOD IDEA TO SERVE THIS SAUCE TO CHILDREN, PREGNANT WOMEN, THE ELDERLY OR ANYONE WITH A WEAKENED IMMUNE SYSTEM.

MAKES ABOUT 135ML/4FL OZ/½ CUP

INGREDIENTS
    115g/4oz/½ cup unsalted
      (sweet) butter
    2 egg yolks
    15–30ml/1–2 tbsp lemon juice,
      white wine vinegar or tarragon
      vinegar
    salt and ground white pepper

COOK'S TIP
Instead of adding the butter to the egg mixture in the bowl, you could put the mixture in a food processor and add the butter through the feeder tube, with the motor running.

1 Melt the butter in a small pan. Put the egg yolks and lemon juice or vinegar in a bowl. Add salt and pepper and whisk until completely smooth.

2 Pour the melted butter in a steady stream on to the egg yolk mixture, beating vigorously with a wooden spoon to make a smooth, creamy sauce. Taste the sauce and add more lemon juice or vinegar if necessary.

MUSTARD AND DILL SAUCE

SERVE THIS FRESH-TASTING SAUCE WITH ANY COLD, SMOKED OR RAW MARINATED SALMON. NOTE THAT IT CONTAINS RAW EGG YOLK, SO, AS WITH HOLLANDAISE SAUCE, IT IS BEST TO AVOID SERVING IT TO CHILDREN, PREGNANT WOMEN, THE ELDERLY OR ANYONE WITH A WEAKENED IMMUNE SYSTEM.

MAKES ABOUT 120ML/4FL OZ/½ CUP

INGREDIENTS
    1 egg yolk
    30ml/2 tbsp brown French mustard
    2.5–5ml/½–1 tsp soft dark brown
      sugar
    15ml/1 tbsp white wine vinegar
    90ml/6 tbsp sunflower or vegetable oil
    30ml/2 tbsp finely chopped fresh dill
    salt and ground black pepper

1 Put the egg yolk in a small bowl and add the mustard with a little soft brown sugar to taste. Beat with a wooden spoon until smooth.

2 Stir in the white wine vinegar, then whisk in the oil, drop by drop at the start, then in a steady stream. As the oil is added, the dressing will start to thicken and emulsify.

3 When the oil has been completely amalgamated, season the sauce with salt and pepper, then stir in the finely chopped dill. Cover and chill for 1–2 hours before serving.

OLIVE OIL, TOMATO <u>AND</u> HERB SAUCE

THIS AROMATIC SAUCE IS SERVED WARM, RATHER THAN HOT, WITH GRILLED OR POACHED SALMON OR TROUT. IT TASTES SO GREAT YOU'LL WANT TO PROVIDE PLENTY OF GOOD BREAD OR BOILED NEW POTATOES TO MOP UP ANY SAUCE REMAINING ON THE PLATE.

MAKES ABOUT 350ML/12FL OZ/1½ CUPS

INGREDIENTS
- 225g/8oz tomatoes
- 15ml/1 tbsp finely chopped shallot
- 2 garlic cloves, finely sliced
- 120ml/4fl oz/½ cup extra virgin olive oil
- 30ml/2 tbsp cold water
- 15ml/1 tbsp lemon juice
- caster (superfine) sugar
- 15ml/1 tbsp chopped fresh chervil
- 15ml/1 tbsp chopped fresh chives
- 30ml/2 tbsp torn fresh basil leaves
- salt and ground black pepper

COOK'S TIP
It is essential to the flavour of this sauce that you use the best quality olive oil.

1 Peel and seed the tomatoes, then cut them into fine dice.

2 Place the shallot, garlic and oil in a small pan over a very gentle heat and allow to infuse for a few minutes. The ingredients should warm through, but definitely not fry or cook.

3 Whisk in the cold water and lemon juice. Remove from the heat and stir in the tomatoes. Add a pinch of salt, pepper and caster sugar, then whisk in the chervil and chives. Leave the sauce to stand for about 10–15 minutes. Reheat gently until just warm, then stir in the basil just before serving.

INDEX